Free Inside
and Out

Free Inside and Out

MARILYN MEBERG
and
LUCI SWINDOLL

Published by
THOMAS NELSON
Since 1798

www.thomasnelson.com

We'd love to hear from you about your experience with this book. Please go to **www.thomasnelson.com/letusknow** for a quick and easy way to give us your feedback.

Love to read? Get excerpts from new books sent to you by email. Join Shelf Life, Thomas Nelson's FREE online book club. Go to **www.thomasnelson.com/shelflife**.

FREE INSIDE AND OUT.

© 2007 Marilyn Meberg and Luci Swindoll.

Published in Nashville, Tennessee by Thomas Nelson, Inc.

Thomas Nelson, Inc. titles may be purchased in bulk for educational, business, fundraising, or sales promotional use. For information, please email SpecialMarkets@ThomasNelson.com.

Unless otherwise indicated, Scripture quotations used in this book are from the Holy Bible, New International Version (NIV). Copyright ©1973, 1978, 1984, International Bible Society. Used by permission of Zondervan.

Other Scripture passages are from the following sources: The King James Version of the Bible (KJV). The Living Bible (TLB), copyright © 1971 by Tyndale House Publishers, Wheaton, Ill. Used by permission. *The Message* (MSG), copyright © 1993. Used by permission of NavPress Publishing Group. New American Standard Bible (NASB), © 1960, 1977 by the Lockman Foundation. The New King James Version (NKJV®), copyright © 1979, 1980, 1982, Thomas Nelson, Inc., Publishers. The Holy Bible, New Living Translation (NLT), copyright © 1996 by Tyndale Charitable Trust. Used by permission of Tyndale House Publishers, Wheaton, Ill.

Library of Congress Cataloging-in-Publication Data

Meberg, Marilyn.
    Freedom inside and out / Marilyn Meberg and Luci Swindoll.
      p. cm.

    ISBN 1-4002-7803-1

    1. Liberty--Religious aspects--Christianity. I. Swindoll, Luci, 1932-
II. Title.
BT810.3.M43 2007
248.4--dc22

2006033598

Printed in the United States of America
07 08 09 10 QW 5

In love, in faith unbroken dwell,
friends radiant and inseparable.
—Rupert Brooke

MARILYN has been my greatest cheerleader ever for freedom on the inside. She's taught me that emotions don't have brains so it's OK to feel my feelings, whether they be sad, mad, glad, or bad. When I've dumped my problems or concerns on her, she's received me with an open mind and heart and encouraged me to continue being totally myself. And through it all, she's made me laugh at life and not take myself too seriously. What a gift! For this and *so much more,* I dedicate this book to her . . . in appreciation for thirty-four years of incredible friendship, freedom, and fun.

—Luci Swindoll

LUCI has been my indefatigable companion in experiencing outside freedom and fun since the days of Noah. One of Luci's most endearing qualities is her quest for a good time. We have made outrageous bets (which I always lose) because she will do anything for a laugh. Because she is so free, there is no concern for the externals of image if the reward of winning includes a meal and a memory. Her carefree freedom is a delight to my soul. So naturally, I dedicate this book to her in tribute to that enviable example of living freely and sharing abundantly.

—Marilyn Meberg

Everything is permissible if God does not exist, and as a result, man is forlorn, because neither within him nor without does he find anything to cling to.
—Jean–Paul Sartre

AUTHORS' NOTE: *Twentieth-century French philosopher Jean–Paul Sartre believed that individuals, possessing free will and therefore personal responsibility, mold themselves by making a choice or taking a side. He said people are free because they* can *do this, and they are in anguish because they* must *do this.*

We believe people are free when they've been set free in Christ . . . and in anguish because either they've never found Him or they're bound by legalism. We hope, in this book, to give you encouragement, motivation, and help in finding and enjoying the freedom God wants you to have, both inside and out.

CONTENTS

PART 1: Free on the Inside
MARILYN MEBERG

1. Knowing Who You Are   3

2. Healing from the Pain of Life   18

3. Getting Beyond Those Old Wounds   28

4. Knowing You Have What It Takes   45

5. Loving Others Unconditionally   60

6. Setting Boundaries When You'd Rather Not   80

Contents

PART 2: Free on the Outside
LUCI SWINDOLL

7. Giving Because You've Been Given To   95

8. Choosing Between Yes and No   108

9. Waiting and Not Waiting   120

10. Receiving More When You Already
    Have Enough   133

11. Knowing Beyond the Shadow of a Doubt   147

12. Splurging in God's Abundant Gifts   159

PART 3: Free to Express Yourself
MARILYN MEBERG and LUCI SWINDOLL

13. Marilyn Asks, "What Does Freedom Mean
    to You, Luci?"   175

14. Luci Asks, "What Does Freedom Mean
    to You, Marilyn?"   190

PART 4: Free for a Lifetime
MARILYN MEBERG and LUCI SWINDOLL

15. Understanding the Bondage of Legalism . . .
    Marilyn Meberg   211

Contents

16. Exchanging the Bondage of Legalism for the
    Liberty of Grace . . . Luci Swindoll   217

Notes   223

PART 1

Free on the Inside

Marilyn Meberg

1

Knowing Who You Are

*Finding freedom by getting to know —
and like—yourself*

An airline booking agent was frantically trying to reroute passengers from a canceled flight. The passenger line was long, and the passengers' patience was short. Suddenly an especially angry man pushed his way to the desk. He slapped his ticket down on the counter and shouted, "I have to be on this flight, and it has to be first class!"

The agent replied, "I'm sorry, sir. These folks are ahead of you in line. As soon as it's your turn, I'll be happy to try to help you. I'm sure we'll be able to work something out."

The angry passenger was unimpressed. He loudly asked the agent, so that the passengers behind him could hear, "Do you have any idea who I am?"

Without a moment's hesitation, the agent looked at him, smiled, and grabbed her public address microphone. "May I have your attention, please?" she began, her voice bellowing throughout the terminal. "We have a passenger here who does not know who he is. If anyone can help him find his identity, please come to gate 17."

The people behind him laughed as well as applauded.

Now, this joke has something to say about something I'm going to say, and it is this: do you know who you are? If you heard the question being bellowed out over a PA system somewhere, could you confidently answer, "I *know* who I am!"?

And just what is the big deal about knowing who we are at the beginning of a book about freedom anyway? Why is it important to know who we are, not just when we're traveling through airports, but also when we're doing anything anywhere, beginning with breathing? Here's the answer in a nutshell: as Christians we are supposed to love as Christ loves us (see John 13:45 and 15:12). We know He loves us so much that, even though He was sinless, He died an agonizing death as the penalty for *our* sins. The amazing truth is, because of His sacrifice, even though we may be arrogant travelers or addle-brained nincompoops or little Miss Goody Two-shoes, our mistakes, whatever they may be, can be forgiven so that nothing stands between us and Jesus's extraordinary gift of eternal life. *That's* how much He loves us.

If He loves us so much, and if we're to love as He loves, then we'd better love ourselves too. And to love ourselves, we need to know ourselves—really know who we are. We need to take an inside look and try to see us as He does.

I love the words Henry Nouwen ascribes to God in *The Road to Daybreak*:

> I am your God. . . . I see all of your actions. And I love you because you are beautiful, made in my own image. . . . Do not judge yourself. . . . Do not condemn yourself . . . Do not reject yourself. . . . Come, come, let me wipe your tears and let my mouth say, "I love you, I love you, I love you."[1]

Those words are not a direct quote from the Bible, but the sentiment is. Jesus is quoted in John 15:9 saying, "I have loved you even as the Father has loved me. Remain in my love" (NLT). Jeremiah 31:3 says, "I have loved you, my people, with an everlasting love. With unfailing love I have drawn you to myself" (NLT).

We are loved!

Why? I don't have a clue. We just are. I guess we'll have to discuss the wisdom of His choice when we meet Him.

In this book, Luci and I want to help you understand

and enjoy the amazing freedom we have in Christ. Everything we'll talk about springs from the foundational, unshakable, unalterable truth that God's love for His creation is tenacious and nonnegotiable. That truth is our most crucial answer to the "Do you know who you are?" question, and it is also the most crucial reality leading us to freedom.

You are loved by the Creator of the universe, and that love sets you free.

WHAT DO YOU HEAR YOURSELF FEELING?

God wills for us to understand and appreciate ourselves to the same degree He appreciates us. To accomplish that, we first need to get acquainted with ourselves as we really are through active self-listening and active self-empathy. We need to press an imaginary stethoscope against our hearts, listening for whatever feelings are inside.

Once we're able to hear and identify those emotional bumps, thumps, and *whoosh*es, the inner harmony that results brings not one but two kinds of amazing freedom. We are freed from the death punishment that came with sin, and for that reason, we are *spiritually* free. But God also wants us to be *emotionally* free, and to accomplish that we have to know who we really are and, no matter what we find, love ourselves as He does.

God loves every facet of who we are, and that includes our sometimes-faltering emotions. To know ourselves and recognize we're still worthy of love in spite of what we see (and what God already knows) is a freedom-from-emotional-bondage moment. That's the moment I hope to lead you to in the pages ahead.

So let's get on with it, shall we? Let's go back to that airport and imagine ourselves assuring our fellow passengers in the frazzled gate agent's line that we do, indeed, know who we are. For example, although it would never happen because I am the height of decorum when I travel, if I were the object of the gate agent's query, and if anyone showed the slightest interest in my identity as he or she waited in line, I could begin by saying I am a Presbyterian who cannot stay with the beat during praise-chorus worship services. While everyone else is clapping and swaying rhythmically, I am wishing we were singing "Shall We Gather at the River" or "Amazing Grace," hymns that allow me to stand still with my hands and arms resting motionlessly at my sides.

If that information aroused even a minimal response, I could follow with the fact that I am mathematically challenged and then share the story problem Mrs. Boden posed to our fourth-grade class that left me in a mindless stare through both reading and recess: "If the temperature is zero outside today and it's going to be twice as cold tomorrow, how cold will it be?"

Perhaps I could get even more personal and say I am an only child and now a widow, and I get lonely sometimes. But in case anyone offered a brother-in-law, cousin, or uncle as a prospective spouse, I could say I'd never consider remarriage unless he were old with a lot of money and a persistent cough. It would also help if he had no kids.

Now, perhaps you're noticing that I'm offering a fascinating recital of some truly mind-numbing facts, yet none of the information I offer the other passengers truly tells them who I am. And reciting those few facts gives no indication that I know who I am either! My self-description has offered only surface snippets of nonessential trivia. I could recite those snippets without ever once turning an imaginary stethoscope inward to hear my interior sounds of vulnerability, hurt, or confusion—if indeed those sounds or feelings are in me. But knowing who we are requires exactly that: active self-listening and active self-empathy. We need to hear what's going on inside ourselves. And no matter what we hear, we need to be kind to ourselves about it.

OPENING THE GATE FOR MY AUTHENTIC SELF

Let me tell you about a recent experience requiring active self-listening and active empathy. It was early evening with a nonintrusive breeze and the makings of a gorgeous Texas sunset. I was sitting on my patio surrounded by beautiful, eagerly blooming petunias and other plants whose names I don't know but whose colors please my soul. My friend Pat Wenger had popped by, and we were both commenting on our budding love of Texas. We had both moved from California, and we considered ourselves reluctant transplants.

My backyard has a wrought-iron fence that runs the length of my property. It is meant to discourage all the ducks, geese, egrets, herons, turtles, and other local creatures whose home is the lake beyond my fence. The wrought iron keeps these wonderful animal friends (most of them anyway) from adopting my yard as a place for private deposits. All my neighbors also have a wrought-iron fence that tells the creatures they need to know their place to the same degree we know ours, but we have the option to look at each other whenever we want to.

As Pat and I were sitting there luxuriating in the beauty of our surroundings, some neighbors from "across the pond" were walking by. I had met them twice the previous summer and found them utterly charming and delightful. So Pat and I walked to the edge of the backyard and leaned over the fence, catching up on the neighborhood doings, with special attention paid to the future of an elusive beaver who sneaks into our lake occasionally. It is common knowledge the beaver has designs on our trees. As a result, the trees all wear wire-mesh panties meant to discourage his attacks. But in spite of our protective efforts, he still occasionally manages to claim the virtue of a tree or two. While we are fascinated by the beaver, his busy endeavors are troubling to us all.

As we moved effortlessly from topic to topic, I got tired of leaning on the fence. I dragged my patio chair down to the fence, sat down, and was much more comfortable. Ultimately the neighbors commented that they needed to "scoot on home." We had been chatting over an hour.

After they'd gone and Pat and I had resumed our places on the patio, she said, "I don't want to put you on the spot, Marilyn, but why didn't you invite those neighbors onto the patio? They stood there for over an hour shifting from foot to foot and swatting mosquitoes while you sat comfortably in your chair."

I was completely taken aback. I thought, *You're right. Why didn't I invite them in?*

Doing so would have meant I had to come into the house and scrounge around for the key to unlock the gate, but surely I could have found it. Why in the world did I just leave them standing outside the gate? Admittedly, we don't know each other well, but what better way to get to know people than to invite them in?

I was at a loss to figure myself out, and I was also embarrassed. Pat wouldn't judge me (well, she did for a minute), but what a lousy impression I must have made on those dear neighbors. Mercy!

See the kinds of disturbing things you can find when you're investigating your innermost thoughts? Whose idea was this stupid stethoscope thing anyway? But here's the deal on the stethoscope: I needed to hear what was going on inside of me. It isn't that I haven't already had a sneaking suspicion that I'm a selfish woman. But the fence-and-chair experience left no wiggle room for argument or doubt. There I sat. There they stood.

So now what? The stethoscope did its job. Now what's *my* job?

My job is to remember that the process of knowing who I am requires active self-listening and active self-empathy. I've done the self-listening. It's time now to do the self-empathy.

THE DIFFERENCE BETWEEN EMPATHY AND SYMPATHY

Before we talk about how we show self-empathy, let me tell you that Luci and I have had any number of discussions on the difference between *empathy* and *sympathy*. Admittedly, by definition, the two words are very similar. *Sympathy* is defined as "a feeling of pity or sorrow for the distress of another person." *Empathy* is "identification with the feelings of another's sorrow or distress."

I maintain in my conversations with Luci that empathy is stronger than sympathy. I can feel sympathy, but that is not as strong as actually identifying with someone. I think sympathy comes with a tiny airbag. Sympathy says, "I feel sorry for you, but I'm separate from you."

On the other hand, when I feel empathy I'm *not* separate from you. I feel your pain because your pain literally becomes my pain. There's no airbag with empathy. With Luci, I get both sympathy and empathy. Whatever I need she gives to me in abundance. And not only that, she has the gift of hospitality. Sigh . . .

OK, so why am I making such a big deal about the word *empathy*? Because I see God all over that word. It was total empathy Jesus showed me when He identified with my sin and went to the cross with it. He literally became sin. His death on the cross for my sin set me free. Because of Jesus, the sin penalty was paid. God was not just sympathetic concerning His wayward creation; He was empathetic.

He continues to be. He will always be.

Now let's take one little step back to remember that we are to love as God loves. I am to love me as God loves me. And how does He love me? Empathetically. That means I love myself the same way, and I treat my emotions with empathic kindness. I don't let myself off the hook after I've taken an inside look to both see and hear what's going on in me, but by the same token I don't beat myself up and dump buckets of condemnation on my head either. Being free in Christ means we've been freed from condemnation. The emancipation proclamation for us as believers is Romans 8:1: "Now there is no condemnation for those who belong to Christ Jesus" (NLT)!

So what does Marilyn do about her issue of selfishness?

She is gently firm. She realizes she needs to change her way of thinking. After that, she needs to begin training herself in new behaviors. She can accomplish that by encouraging herself to develop "new ways" of doing things and being patient with herself when she forgets that you might want a chair too.

Being empathic with myself means I show kindness toward myself by identifying with my weaknesses (in this case, selfishness) and knowing my behaviors can be changed if I commit myself to making that change.

GETTING RID OF THE AIRBAG

Here's another clarifying dimension of self-empathy: empathy means *fully identifying* what's going on inside us. We often distance ourselves from our authentic self because it's easier to deny being selfish than to admit to

it. We don't want to feel depressed about our real inclinations and patterns, so we pretend those inclinations
don't exist. That is separating; that's placing a little airbag between the real me and the denying me. I should
not separate from myself when I find that self to have
unattractive and embarrassing behaviors. Doing so
means I have to perform a cover-up to keep the denying
self from finding out what the blabbermouth true self is
trying to reveal.

Get rid of the airbag! How? By listening to your true
self. When we listen to ourselves, the airbag disappears.
We identify with our own weakness instead of denying
it exists. Work toward better thinking and better behavior, and as you do, you'll enjoy internal unity . . . inner
harmony . . . *emotional freedom.*

So where does this inner blabbermouth come from,
and why is it so relentlessly determined to help us get
rid of the airbag of self-denial? Why can't it just allow us
to separate from ourselves and/or be crabby with ourselves when we want to be? Why won't it leave us alone
to be phony if we feel like it? *Why doesn't it just be quiet?*

Actually we *can* get it to be quiet . . . by being louder
than it is.

Let's switch gears for just a minute and talk about our
need for noise. You've undoubtedly noticed our culture is
becoming increasingly noisy. Many of us frequently have
gadgets in our ears—cell phones or iPods or other high-

tech devices—that send sound directly into our brains. In our homes, the television is often on, even if no one is watching, because we need noise in our environment. And just imagine how uncomfortable an elevator would be if we did not have the distraction of elevator music. We might hear someone's stomach gurgling or perhaps even more organic noises than that! "Spare us that social connection," we say. "Crank up the music."

The fact is, most of us flee total silence. It is unsettling to us because many of us are trying hard to hide under blankets of activity and sound. Maybe we can drown out the inner blabbermouth if we can surround ourselves with noise and distraction. And without that inner blabbermouth, we won't have to think, feel, or confront as long as the racket is coming from somewhere.

Just what *is* that inner blabbermouth? Is it friend or foe? It's friend. It's a friend determined to produce inner harmony. Without sounding disrespectful, the fact is, the blabbermouth voice is placed there by God. He wills for us to have congruence. Which brings us back to my statement at the beginning of this discussion: God wants us to understand and appreciate ourselves to the *same* degree He appreciates us—and He's crazy about us! When we accomplish the inner harmony He wants us to have, we find the freedom He wants us to enjoy. And the first step of that process is active self-listening and active self-empathy.

FLINGING OPEN THE GATE

So now that I have listened to my inner self and identified my tendency to think of my own needs before the needs of others, and recognizing the root of my preferences as selfishness, is God disgusted with me? Amazingly enough, He isn't. Will He walk away and leave me selfishly keeping all my chairs for myself? Never. He provides me with the grace to work on my humanity without condemning me for it.

How about my neighbors? How am I going to show them I am a reformed woman capable of unselfish acts? I haven't seen them since that evening, but you can bet the crown on your lower-left molar I now know exactly where my gate key is. If I see them coming, the gate will be flung open. As they sit down on my patio chairs, perhaps registering slightly bewildered expressions, I'll offer them coffee, with or without cream, and hope to goodness no one says anything interesting until I get back. Maybe I should offer them cold water instead of hot coffee so I won't be in the kitchen as long.

AFTERTHOUGHT

Luci thinks my imaginary stethoscope sounds a little spooky. Her comment was, "Marilyn, you make that thing sound like some sort of magic connector to our thoughts. I think that's a little weird! I know you're using the stethoscope simply as a visual aid to the reader to communicate the fact that we can access our thoughts if we look and listen to our inner being, but quite frankly, it makes me want to avoid stethoscopes. When Dr. Moore makes a move to listen to the number of heartbeats I have per minute, I'm going to tell her to guess. How do I know how much private information that thing might give away while she pretends to be listening to my heart?"

I just love it when Luci gets the point.

2

Healing from the Pain of Life

Remembering God's love
when hard things happen

When our daughter, Beth, reluctantly started kinder-garten many years ago, she found herself increasingly enthusiastic about school because of Harvey Barencloft's attentions to her. Every day he would bring a little treat for her from his mother's kitchen. The treats would range from homemade chocolate chip cookies or little bags of potato chips to brownies or, one day, a bag of radishes.

They would sit under a tree during recess, munch their treats, and chat. One of Beth's favorite topics was Harvey's expressions of love for her. He loved her red hair, her dark brown eyes, and that she thought "deep thoughts."

Apparently one of her deep thoughts was expressed by the question, "Why do you think God made radishes?"

The sweet kinship between Beth and Harvey began to lessen shortly before Christmas. Beth didn't understand why he seemed to prefer playing soccer at recess instead of sitting with her under the "munching tree." He continued to be nice to her, but apparently his mother's pantry was bare. No more treats ... no more chats ... and then ... no more boyfriend. Harvey Barencloft found a new woman. Beth saw them under the munching tree eating things out of a Baggie. Apparently his mother's pantry had been replenished. Beth was crushed.

I took Beth's loss hard. I hated seeing her sad little face each morning as she trudged off to school. I even went so far as to ask if she'd like me to send a little Baggie of radishes with her. "No, Mama," she answered sadly. "The only good thing about no more chats under the munching tree is I don't have to pretend I like radishes. But mostly, Mama, I know I will never get over this. It's too big for my heart."

I was stricken. I well remember my own all-consuming crush on Anthony Farenheight in the third grade. When he chose Darlene Zapholny as my replacement, I also thought I would never recover. But I did. And Beth did. Life went on, and more boys entered and then left the love cycle. Last night, thirty-three years after Harvey Barencloft, I was chatting with Beth on the phone. I asked her if she remembered Harvey and the heart-hurt he had inflicted on her in kindergarten. She paused for several seconds and then said, "I haven't eaten a radish since."

IN OUR PAIN, FINDING MEANING AND PURPOSE

Pain experienced at any age can feel at times too large for our heart's ability to recover. It is not uncommon for us to whisper to ourselves, "I'll never get over this . . . I'll never be the same . . . I don't think I'm going to survive." It's also not uncommon for us to be leveled by the senselessness of our pain. We ask, "Why did this happen? What is the point? This makes no sense. Everything was going well until . . ." Most of us can't help wondering, *If God loves me so much, why did He let this happen to me? Why has He let me go through so much pain?*

As Viktor Frankl endured multiple atrocities during his confinement in a Nazi death camp, he came to realize that the prisoners who had a sense of purpose maintained a will to live. Later, upon liberation from the camp, Frankl wrote the now-classic book *Man's Search for Meaning*. In that book he encourages all people to find personal purpose for their existence on the earth. With that purpose will come meaning for their experiences.

For example, I was heartened to read the story of Laurie Johnson, who lost her husband and twenty-three-month-old son in a small-plane crash. That same accident left her on crutches with a crushed leg as well as nearly unbearable pain. Her heartbreaking loss and pain caused Laurie to descend into a vacuum of deep depression. She feared she would never walk normally again, and she knew the loss of her husband and baby boy would prevent her from ever living normally again.

One day, in an effort to lift her spirits, Laurie's older sister trimmed her crutches' hand and armpit pads with leopard-print fabric. Laurie says that crazy fabric was a ray of fun for her in an otherwise sad existence. Now, three years later, she has attached meaning and purpose to her experience in a surprising way. She has established the first line of designer crutches; they are sold on the Internet and have proven to be a source of encouragement to many with physical disabilities. One woman claims she changes the covers on her crutches like other people change their shoes.

But the crutches are more than a fun fashion item. Fifty percent of the proceeds go toward a nonprofit foundation for people who have lost multiple family members. Laurie decided she needed to find meaning as well as purpose in her loss, and she did so in a wonderfully creative way.

Her physical and emotional wounds may have healed, but her scars remind her always of those who have a similar need for encouragement in their losses.

CAN WE *REALLY* HEAL FROM LIFE'S PAIN?

As long as we live in this imperfect place, we are going to experience pain. If you ask me whether anyone ever gets well from that pain, my answer is a qualified yes. It's qualified because, since pain is inevitable in our broken world, we will *always* be in the process of seeking recovery from it. Undergirding our recovery work, however, is a sovereign and loving God who promises to hear us in our pain and give us the tools we need to survive. He's been keeping that promise since He created us. Psalm 138:3 states, "When I called, you answered me; you made me bold and stouthearted." I love that! I love knowing I can be "bold and stouthearted" with God's help. And Psalm 17:6 also reassures us with these words: "I call on you, O God, for you will answer me; give ear to me and hear my prayer."

We feel incredible encouragement to our souls when we know the pain of our life is known to God and that He is not indifferent to that pain. If we think He does not care and is indifferent to the excesses of our struggle, we lose hope—not only for ourselves but for life itself. Such was the case for Elie Wiesel, who was a teenager when he and his family were routed from their home in 1944 and taken to the Auschwitz concentration camp and then on to Buchenwald. His book *Night* is a terrifying account of his memories of those camps.

Wiesel says he will never forget those moments that

murdered His God and turned his dreams to ashes. He asked his father, as the black smoke from burning bodies filled the air, how such a thing could be happening. It was the twentieth century, he reasoned. Who would allow such crimes to be committed? How could the world remain silent?

As a committed Jew, Wiesel was trained in the meaning of the Psalms, and yet he felt no sense that God gave him His ear or that He answered his prayers. Such spiritual despair gave way to total disbelief in a caring God as Wiesel witnessed the cruel death of his father. No loving God could just stand by and watch such horrors without intervening, Wiesel thought. He vowed never again to speak to such a God.

Wiesel survived the Nazi camps and was freed from its demonic tyranny at the end of World War II. His survival was not a miracle, he said; it was nothing more than chance. He was weak, shy, and did nothing to save himself. But having survived, he felt the need to give meaning to his survival.

In his 1986 Nobel Peace Prize acceptance speech, Wiesel stated how he does just that:

I swore never to be silent whenever and wherever human beings endure suffering and humiliation. We must take sides. Neutrality helps the oppressor, never the victim. Silence encourages the tormenter, never the tormented. Sometimes we must interfere. When human lives are endangered, when human dignity is in jeopardy, national borders and sensitivities become irrelevant. Wherever men and women are persecuted because of their race, religion, or political views, that place must at that moment become the center of the universe.[1]

Wiesel believes that, as a witness to the horrors of the Nazi concentration camps, he has a moral obligation to try to prevent the enemy from enjoying one last victory by having its crimes erased from human memory. He cannot let that happen, so he must write his legacy of words and memories to prevent history from repeating itself. That work has given meaning to his suffering and purpose to his life.

At some point in Wiesel's post-camp recovery time, I believe he reconnected to the God he had rejected as uncaring and indifferent. At some point he received the hope of a God he could call on, a God who will answer him, give ear to him, and hear his prayer. My assumption is based on these words from his Nobel Prize speech:

I have faith. Faith in the God of Abraham, Isaac, and Jacob, and even in His creation. Without it no action would be possible. And action is the only remedy to indifference, the most insidious danger of all.[2]

Although Wiesel believed his survival was merely chance, I have to disagree. Seen through the grid of God's sovereign design, I don't think there was anything "chance" about it. I don't pretend to understand why others were incinerated and he was not, but it is obvious his voice is needed in a world still filled with terror and violence. He is the author of more than forty internationally acclaimed works of fiction and nonfiction, and in addition to the Nobel Prize, he has been awarded the Presidential Medal of Freedom and the U.S. Congressional Gold Medal, and he has been honored by the French Legion of Honor. Today Wiesel maintains, "One person of integrity can make a difference, a difference of life and death."[3] His voice is making a difference in a world God cares about because he found meaning in his pain and purpose in his life.

THE GRID OF GOD'S SOVEREIGN DESIGN

We *can* heal from life's painful experiences; we *can* get better, but not without participating in the recovery process. A part of that process is attaching some kind of meaning to our hurtful experiences. Doing so is not only practical, it's biblical. Everything we experience in life travels first through the grid of God's sovereign design.

Tragic experiences that at first mystify us and hurt us

may even cause our faith to tremble. Remembering that God is in control of all things and that all things work together for our good helps us more easily participate in the process of recovering from pain. Why? Because we're comforted to know God is always there whether or not we feel His presence.

Remember the Old Testament Joseph, whose brothers sold him into slavery? He experienced years of emotional and physical pain from the injustices heaped upon him. He was an innocent man, yet he suffered for no discernable reason. At the time the hardships were happening, he could not have attached meaning to those heartrending experiences. They must have seemed totally senseless. But in time Joseph saw what God was doing, and that understanding freed him from bitterness and despair. Later he would tell his brothers,

> Do not be distressed and do not be angry with yourselves for selling me here, because it was to save lives that God sent me ahead of you. For two years now there has been famine in the land, and for the next five years there will not be plowing and reaping. But God sent me ahead of you to preserve for you a remnant on earth and to save your lives by a great deliverance.
>
> So then, it was not you who sent me here but God. (Genesis 45:5–8)

OUR JOB, GOD'S PURPOSE

Knowing a fully participating God is working in the events of my life is enormously healing. I need to do what I can in making sense of it all, which includes giving those events meaning. But my job also is to trust God's character and purpose for my life as His sovereign design is established. Ephesians 1:4–5 clearly states God's purpose for the world: "Long before he laid down earth's foundations, he had us in mind, had settled on us as the focus of his love. . . . Long, long ago he decided to adopt us into his family through Jesus Christ" (MSG).

What a liberating message! We're in God's family. He loves us no matter what we find inside ourselves when we fully learn who we are. He is not indifferent to what happens to us, and He does not judge us when we feel weak in our faith and dare to ask, "What are You doing?" and *"Why* are You doing this?"

His Word assures us He ordains healing for our wounds. But for those times when the meaning of tragic and trying experiences is totally unclear and we're hurt that God allowed them, we need to remind ourselves of this powerfully simple directive in Proverbs 3:5: "Trust in the LORD with all your heart and lean not on your own understanding."

Freedom comes from trusting.

3

Getting Beyond Those Old Wounds

Escaping the prison of past fears,
flaws, abuses, grief, and loss

This morning as I was walking into my bank to deposit my widow's mite the manager came striding out of his office, throwing behind him the words, "I'm not going, and I told him I'm not going."

Since we were on the verge of colliding, I felt constrained to make him aware of my presence. "I'm not going either," I said. "In fact, I don't know anyone who *is* going!"

He stopped dead in his tracks, recognized me, and laughed that chipmunk laugh that always catches me off guard. "You make my day, Marilyn," he said. "What is it with you?"

I would have been happy to explain that what it is with me is that I am mildly insane, but he turned and continued going wherever he was going—or not going. I guess the "What is it with you?" question was not meant to receive an answer. But it has stayed with me for quite some time, and even though you probably haven't spouted off at me with some nonsensical wisecrack, as I did the bank manager, it prompts me now to ask you the same question: what's up with *you*?

☺ *Giggle Break* ☺

Due to my previously confessed affliction with mild insanity, I tend to occasionally lapse into unexpected bouts of foolishness, and I feel one coming on now. So before we get into the rewarding work of finding out what it is with you, let's take a little giggle break. What I'm about to share with you has absolutely nothing to do with what we're talking about. For some odd reason, that pleases me; such is the nature of insanity, I suppose. So here's the giggle:

Mama had four wonderful sons who became successful professionals and made a lot of money.

One evening the brothers were discussing what kind of gift each could give to their mother. She was elderly and lived several hundred miles away from the boys. They were eager to show their appreciation of her. So they shared gift ideas and soon set about delivering them.

Sometime later, the brothers got together again and discussed the gift each had given Mama. The first brother said, "I had a huge house built for her."

The second said, "I had a hundred-thousand-dollar theater built in the house."

The third said, "I had my Mercedes dealer deliver an SL600 to her."

The fourth said, "Knowing how Mama loves to read Scripture, and knowing her eyesight is failing, I bought a parrot that can recite the entire Bible. All Mama has to do is name the chapter and verse, and the parrot will recite it. Of course, the bird cost me a fortune—two hundred thousand dollars—but I think it will be perfect for Mama's needs."

The other brothers were impressed. Soon Mama sent each son a thank-you note. She wrote:

"John, the house you built is so huge I live in only one room but still have to clean the whole house. Thanks anyway."

"James, you gave me an expensive theater that can hold fifty people, but I'm so old all my friends are dead. I've lost my hearing, and I'm nearly blind, so I'll never use it. But thanks anyway."

"Jim, I am too old to travel. I stay home, and I have my groceries delivered. So I never use the Mercedes. But thanks anyway."

"Dearest Jack, you were the only son to have the good sense to give a little thought to your gift. The chicken was delicious. Thank you."

CONTINUING TOWARD FREEDOM

As you may know, I'm a strong believer in the healing power of laughter. All laughter has healing properties for the body and the soul, so it's an antidote for life's stresses, and we want to use it as often as possible. That's why I like to throw out frivolous funnies now and then. Humor is especially helpful when we're confronting challenging issues, as we'll be doing in this chapter. So now that we've had our giggle break, let's get back to the rewarding work of setting our inner self free.

I hope by now you are completely assured that God is crazy about you. I hope you've learned to use your imaginary stethoscope to investigate the thoughts and feelings in your authentic self so you know who you are. And most importantly, I hope you know that, no matter what you find in this ongoing, ultrapersonal investigation, God's love remains constant.

If you are certain of God's love, uncertainty slinks out the side door, and once it has made its exit, you are free to enjoy the spiritually and emotionally abundant life God wants you to have. In chapter 2, we built upon your certainty of God's love by discussing how it supports you in healing from painful experiences as you find meaning in your pain and purpose in your life. But maybe, as you've been listening to your innermost self with that imaginary stethoscope, you have discovered some old wounds that still cause pain. In this chapter I want to discuss how we can get beyond those old wounds that won't go away and how, as we do so, we come closer to fully experiencing the freedom God wants us to have.

WOUNDS INFLICTED BY UNSPOKEN MESSAGES

Sometimes we feel emotional wounds that don't seem to heal, and we aren't sure why they continue to cause us pain. I have a dear friend who struggles with this kind of wound. She is a "sigher." When she is especially stressed, she sighs more frequently and more audibly. When I had the audacity once to ask her, "If that sigh had a voice, what would it be saying?" she was startled by my question. She had not heard herself sigh.

Ultimately she realized she had a years-long history of sighing. One day, after some weeks of reflection, she said, "I'll tell you what my sigh is saying; it's saying, 'You aren't going to make it.'"

We talked about the "it" she was not going to make, and she realized "it" was anything that felt too hard to accomplish, was impossible to avoid, or brought up her constant fear of failure. That "it" was caused by old, emotional wounds that wouldn't heal, wounds that had dogged her footsteps all her life and caused her to become a sigher. Once she heard and acknowledged what her sighs were "saying," she could work on getting past those old wounds.

My sighing friend, whom I will call Gail, was reared by a single mother who was exceedingly protective and fear-prone. Gail was not allowed to walk to school (three blocks) because "something" might happen. When Gail was old enough to drive, her mother would not let her get a driver's license because "something" might happen. Nor was Gail allowed to go away to college because, again, "something" might happen. As a result, Gail lived at home until she was twenty-six with her mother driving her wherever she needed to go. Gail never felt competent to do things for herself because (surely without meaning to) her mother had taught her it would be best if Mother did whatever needed to be done.

When Gail's mother died unexpectedly of a heart attack, Gail was devastated. Suddenly there was no one to make decisions for her, no one to protect her from the "something" that might happen. It was a tremendously difficult time, but gradually Gail recovered, at least to a degree. Eventually she met and then married a wonderfully kind and sensitive man. She was drawn to him because he was strong and seemed always to know what to do. In his sensitivity, he also encouraged her to grow and develop her interior being.

Gail was afraid to work outside the home, and she and her husband never had children. She told me she was sure she would be a "terrible mother." But she was a talented gardener and a fantastic cook, and no one ever wanted to miss one of her dinner parties. Not only was the food incomparable, so too were the flower arrangements fresh from Gail's garden.

Gail's "old wounds" were inflicted as she grew up listening to the inner messages delivered by her mother: *You can't do it . . . You're not strong enough . . . You're not smart enough . . . You're not mature enough.* Gail's mother did not knowingly cripple Gail's emotional development. She didn't actually say those messages aloud, but the implication was always there. The message was that unless Mother did it, it could not be accomplished because Gail lacked competence.

For a long time, Gail's own wounds continued to enslave her. But now she has found the courage to recognize them, and she's working on getting past them. With good therapy, she's beginning to realize how those incompetence messages shaped her childhood self-evaluations and followed her right on into adulthood. Of course, now Gail is furious with her mother, but she'll work through that. In time she will come to realize her mother was an emotional cripple herself and did not intentionally set out to cripple Gail. Her mother was simply living out her own incompetence. Gail's next task will be to forgive her mother for what she did not realize what she was doing.

Gail has not stopped sighing, but she does it less frequently and less audibly. Healing from her woundedness is coming as she realizes she is not an inferior or incompetent woman. She is also experiencing healing as she understands more and more the heart of God. He has never viewed her as inadequate. He has equipped her with the capability to grow into a full understanding of her God-given abilities. She has a part-time job now working in the cosmetics area of a major department store. No one but God, her husband, and Gail know what a miracle that is.

Gail's new life today is another example of how freedom accompanies an "inside look." She now knows who she really is, knows without question that God loves her, and is learning how to find meaning and purpose in life's pain and get beyond the old wounds. In doing this work, she also has become increasingly aware of an internal freedom previously unknown to her. God willed that freedom for her. He wills it for all of us. Galatians 5:1 tells us, "Christ has set us free to live a free life" (MSG).

WRAPPING OURSELVES IN WOUNDWART

Bear with me, please, as we do a seemingly abrupt change of subject that I hope will eventually make sense: have you ever heard of "woundwart"? I hadn't, but I happened to come across it in the dictionary, and I love the peculiar images the word brings to mind. In case you share my ignorance, woundwart is not an extra-strength skin irritation caused by handling toads, but a plant, or a category of plants, all of which have long, downy leaves. These leaves were once used to treat wounds.

That's the extent of my information, sparingly provided by the dictionary. My imagination supplies the rest, creating in my mind an image of severely injured people wrapped up in long woundwart leaves waiting for healing to occur. It makes sense that their wound-wart bandages would need to be changed from time to time. Do you suppose the injured persons had to venture out in search of more woundwart plants when that need arose, or could a supply be kept in someone's pantry? It certainly gives one pause to wonder (perhaps wondering, while one is at it, whether the mild insanity I claim to have has, in fact, reached a more advanced state).

So OK, Marilyn, what's your point? My point originally was to talk about the word *wound*; then I discovered *woundwart*, and it was simply too fascinating not to share. But now I'm back on track, back to the word *wound* and the fact that this chapter is about getting beyond old wounds.

The dictionary defines a wound as "a break in the skin" or "a mental or emotional blow." Thus, a wound is an injury that has yet to heal. All wounds, even small ones, can be potentially dangerous because of the possibility of infection. And this is true of both physical and emotional wounds. If we say we have a broken heart, we are saying we've endured a hurtful experience that has injured us emotionally, and that wound has yet to heal. Like physical wounds, emotional wounds also are vulnerable to "infection" that prolongs the hurt. We need to be mindful of our emotional wounds and sensitive to how they may continue to hurt us long after the injurious experience has passed.

A WOUND THAT LINGERS

Am I suggesting that deep emotional wounds will never heal? As a former mental-health professional, I certainly do not believe that. Old wounds *can* heal. I have seen them heal; I am watching Gail heal. I have also experienced the healing of some of my own wounds. But I also have seen and personally experienced some wounds that remain wounds.

Let me illustrate by making a distinction between a wound and a scar. A scar covers what was once a wound. Before the scar appeared, a scab formed over the wound to protect it while it healed. Once that healing occurred, the scab fell off, leaving behind the scar.

Many of us have been wounded and have the scars to prove it. We have healed, but our scars remind us that we have been wounded. Remembering an emotional hurt is like seeing a physical scar. We don't forget, but neither do we bleed anymore. There is no longer a wound in need of woundwart. There is, instead, a scar.

On the other hand, there are some wounds that do not heal, wounds that still bleed. For me, these are wounds for which I prowl around in the dead of night in search of woundwart. Many years after the emotional wound was inflicted, I still do not anticipate a scar ever forming. Let me tell you about one of them.

Prior to the death of my husband, Ken, from pancreatic

cancer, I anticipated we would at some point have a wrap-it-all-up-in-a-bow chat. I wanted to reminisce about the many funny and good times we had enjoyed, like the Maude Amy–Gollius Gullah skits we performed for parties. I wanted to apologize (again) for that hitchhiking stunt of mine at my fortieth birthday party. I wanted him to know there was not a man on the planet with whom I would rather have shared my life. I wanted to tell him our kids had a gazillion reasons to be as proud of their dad as I was. I wanted him to know he made the best country-style spareribs in the entire state of California. I wanted to giggle again over why we had shared the world's worst honeymoon. I wanted to tell him (again) I never should have begged for that Fiat convertible. And I wanted to thank him (again) for getting it for me anyway.

The list of things I wanted to chat about was long. The list was never communicated.

Why? Because Ken didn't want to do it. He had always hated good-byes, and a "wrap-it-all-up-in-a-bow" good-bye was too big for him to talk about. So, at his request, we never did. I certainly had no right to force such an exchange on him. I wanted to honor his wishes in any way I could. But in doing so, my heart wound has never healed. I'm not mad at him; I'm not blaming him. I just wish we could have had that final good-bye chat. There was stuff I wanted to say—and stuff I wanted to hear.

Because I didn't get to say or hear that stuff, I live with an old wound that won't heal.

RECOGNIZING OLD WOUNDS

Emotional wounds *can* heal, but many of them don't. It is possible, however, even essential, that we learn how to keep those chronic hurts from imprisoning us in misery. The first step in doing that is recognizing we have them.

For me, these wounds are revealed by what I think of as "internal bleeding." This is an emotion different from being sad, different from experiencing loss. It is simply a quiet pain that does not go away. I am living my life with enthusiasm, purpose, and gratitude. But always I'm aware of my need for an occasional wrap in wound-wart. Is that OK, or is it a sign I'm resisting a process that is supposed to take away the occasional bleeding of this old wound?

To answer, let me take a step back and recap how far we've come in this book intended to help you find freedom inside and out. I've suggested we begin this freedom work by getting to know our authentic self, listening to our innermost thoughts, and learning to love ourselves as God loves us. In the knowing and listening, we acknowledge the painful experiences we've endured. We heal from those experiences by finding meaning in them, and even when that meaning remains elusive, we trust that whatever has happened to us has come through the grid of God's design for our lives. Trusting that His love for us is constant, we build purpose into the way we live.

But even when we've progressed this far in our work toward "inside" freedom, we may continue to live with hurtful wounds that threaten to re-infect us with emotional bondage long past the actual experience. Gail was held in bondage to old wounds that would not heal. Through therapy she identified those wounds, which she previously had not even recognized, and she is continuing her work in getting beyond them. It's unclear at this point whether the wounds will heal into scars or continue to occasionally bleed as wounds that won't heal. Either way, she is moving beyond them.

Gail's mother unconsciously caused her to be shackled by a continual fear of incompetence in the face of the impossible "it." Now Gail is learning to trust in and be confident about her abilities, and as a result, the shackles of the impossible "it" are dropping off as she identifies and challenges those old feelings. She has found meaning in her painful experiences, and as of this writing, is applying to assist in a remedial-reading program for middle-school students. She told me if those kids are suffering from a reading "it," she wants to help them. As she encourages them to believe they can do "it," her life will take on new purpose. So even if the painful experiences she has endured refuse to be covered over with scars, even if her feelings toward her mother continue to bleed occasionally as wounds that will not heal, Gail is moving beyond them. She recognizes that occasional pain is a part of living in an imperfect world, and she no longer lets those old wounds hold her back.

If I were to ask Gail, "What is it with you?" I know what her response would be. She'd probably sigh (confidently this time) and say, "I'm tackling the 'its' in my mind, and I'm winning!" She'd also say she's never felt freer in her life.

LIVING FREELY DESPITE AN IMPERFECT WORLD

Both Gail and I have old wounds that refuse to heal, but we do not let those wounds deprive us of joyful freedom in Christ. We're aware our lives are precious to Him, old wounds and all. We accept that ours is an imperfect world, and for many of us, that means living with wounds that do not heal. We know we have them. We expect them to bleed occasionally. But we don't let them prevent us from having meaningful lives full of purpose.

There are plenty of biblical precedents for this kind of joyful living despite chronic wounds. Consider the meaning and purpose in the life of the apostle Paul, who prayed for the removal of the "thorn in his flesh." The "thorn" remained. And so did Paul's steadfast faith and mighty work on behalf of the gospel.

God does not make our world perfect. That's coming in another life. But freedom *is* available in *this* life. Like the painful experiences we discussed in chapter 2, our wounds that do not heal may simply be the stuff of human existence. If we've looked at them and brought them to the light of divine scrutiny and human intervention, we've done our part. We can trust God to do His, lifting us over those old hurts and helping us live freely beyond them.

I do not let my old wounds deprive me of joyful freedom in Christ; I'm aware my life is precious to Him, old wounds and all, and I'm determined to enjoy every moment of it. So the next time my bank manager goes skidding past me asking, "What is it with you, Marilyn?" I may just say to his retreating back, "Ever heard of woundwart?"

AFTERTHOUGHT

Luci has served as human woundwart for me many times. She knew and loved Ken as he knew and loved her. She was an integral part of our family as our children, Jeff and Beth, were growing up. Sometimes a wound that does not heal needs simply to be allowed to bleed in the presence of someone who knows, cares, and does not judge, and who joins us in occasionally recalling sweet and shared memories.

For me, that means remembering the time Luci and Ken sang "Marilyn's Forty" to the tune of "Alleluia" about every five minutes at my birthday party in a restaurant, with Ken using great conducting flourishes as he invited others to join in. Even when we got back home for games, the two of them continued to repeatedly break into that chorus. As the evening wore on, they began to lose their pitch but not their enthusiasm. And I did not lose my appreciation for their wonderfully zany spirit.

Good times need to be remembered; it's comforting to the wound.

4

Knowing You Have What It Takes

Understanding the gift
God has given you

Do you ever wonder what you're made of? By that I mean, how strong, how resilient, how courageous you would be if your life suddenly took a left turn. Do you wonder the degree to which you would rise to the occasion and fight the circumstances that threaten to defeat you?

Winston Churchill said, "There is only one answer to defeat, and that is victory." We can agree with his premise, but do we have what it takes to defy defeat? Do we have what it takes to press on to victory?

Some of us may let such questions, in various forms,

bind us in perpetual worry and fear of the future. In the previous chapter, for example, we saw how Gail's mother's fear that something bad might happen ultimately locked Gail in a prison of near helplessness.

The fact is, something bad inevitably happens to all of us at one time or another. But an interesting thing happens along with the bad thing. In the experience of enduring a setback, or even a calamity, we find out what we're made of. As some anonymous sage said, "Adversity introduces a person to herself." Aldous Huxley, not content to be anonymous, said, "Experience is not what happens to a person. It is what a person does with what happens to her." (I've taken the liberty of changing the pronouns in these statements to make them more to my liking as well as closer to my gender.) The bottom-line message here is, You don't know what you're made of until forced by circumstances to find out. Then you watch yourself to see what you do.

In this chapter, I want to help you see that, as a child of God and beloved follower of Jesus Christ, you have what it takes to survive any challenge that confronts you and any calamity that befalls you. That's an extraordinary statement but one I truly believe. When you also believe it, you can enjoy life amazingly free of the fear that bad "somethings" may happen to you in the future.

WOMEN WHO HAVE WHAT IT TAKES

I was inspired by the story of Army National Guard Maj. Tammy Duckworth, who found out what she was made of on November 12, 2004. Tammy was at the controls of her Black Hawk helicopter, ferrying troops and supplies throughout the countryside around the tactical operations center at Camp Anaconda near Balad, Iraq, when a rocket-propelled grenade tore through the helicopter floor and exploded in the cockpit, instantly severing her right leg just below the hip.

Tammy's training clicked in, obliterating fear and pain as she consumed herself with trying to land the helicopter without crashing, not realizing her copilot had already taken control. As soon as the craft safely touched down, she passed out. When she awoke several days later at Walter Reed Army Medical Center in Maryland, she had lost both legs. Doctors had managed to salvage her badly injured right arm.

Tammy's recovery was long and arduous, including five hours of exhausting therapy each day to restore movement to her damaged arm and strengthen the muscles that support her leg prostheses. Today she is walking with canes and is determined one day to get back into her copter and fly again. And as of this writing, she is running for Congress from the Illinois Sixth District.

When the rocket-propelled grenade hit Tammy's

helicopter, her life took a dramatic left turn. Since then she has endured tremendous pain, both physical and psychological. She could choose to live as a victim of her life's harsh circumstances. Instead, she has the attitude of a determined survivor. She says she does not worry about what cannot be controlled but instead tries to focus on what can be fixed. She expects someday to retire with her husband in Hawaii, where she plans to go to the beach in a bikini and prostheses with painted toenails.

This little lady is made of sturdy stuff! She has claimed victory over the life wounds that threatened to defeat her.

Another courageous woman who chose victory over defeat and daily shows what she's made of is Minnesota State Senator Mee Moua. She is the first member of the Laotian Hmong tribe to be elected to a state legislature in the United States.

One might never have anticipated such a future for a little girl who in 1975 fled the Laotian Communists with her parents and two siblings. With nothing but the clothes they wore, they walked for nineteen days until they reached the Thai border. For three years they lived in a refugee camp with no electricity, sewers, or running water. Finally a family-reunification program sent them to Mee's grandparents in America.

Mee entered the fourth grade at a Catholic school in Appleton, Wisconsin. It was 1979, not long after the

Vietnam War, and Mee and her family became targets of anti-Asian discrimination and acts of hatred. Their house was egged, kids wrote ugly words on their garage, human excrement was thrown on their lawn, and little Mee was spit at as she walked to school. Now a naturalized citizen, Mee still gets hate mail from people who think she has no right to fly the flag and that her job as a state senator should be held by a "real" American, not a "foreigner."

Mee says that growing up as an immigrant and struggling to master the English language caused her to fight hard to earn respect from her classmates. She joined the Girl Scouts, and for each badge her friends mastered, she got three. She excelled at soccer, became the editor of the high-school newspaper, acted in plays, and competed on the debate team.

She earned a BA on scholarship from Brown University, a master's degree in public affairs from the University of Texas, and a law degree from the University of Minnesota. Not bad for a kid who at one time had fractured English and was considered an outsider by her peers!

Mee is described now as a tireless champion of the disadvantaged: the old, the poor, the sick, and the young. Not surprising, she specializes in immigration law, with a vision of what she wants the world to be.

What is it in people like Mee and Tammy that gives them "what it takes"? What is it about people who refuse to allow their lives not to work? Why do some rise up out of the ghetto of overwhelming odds, defying defeat and persevering until they know victory? The "experts" do not provide a consensus answer to this question, thus giving rise to the familiar nurture-versus-nature debate: is it in the DNA, or is it in the environment?

While I'm not (quite) audacious enough to suggest I know the answer to this question, I do have an opinion, and it is this: in seeking to know how one survives, and even thrives, despite challenging circumstances, we have to consider DNA, early environment, and more importantly, God's sovereign design. Without a doubt, I know He uses both DNA and our environment, as He uses everything He chooses to use, for His sovereign purpose.

☺ *Giggle Break* ☺

Are you ready for another totally non sequitur giggle break? I am! Please bear with me . . .

A teenage boy had just gotten his driving permit. He asked his father, a minister, if they could talk about the use of the car. His father took him to his study and said, "I'll make a deal with you. You bring your grades up, study your Bible more, and get your hair cut. If you can do that, we can talk."

After about a month the boy came back and again asked his father if they could discuss his using the car. They again went to the father's study, where the father said, "Son, I've been real proud of you. You have brought your grades up, and you've been studying your Bible, but you haven't gotten your hair cut."

The boy waited a minute and said, "You know, Dad, I've been thinking about that. With all due respect, may I remind you Samson had long hair, Moses had long hair, and even Jesus had long hair."

His father answered, "That's true, son, and they walked everywhere they went."

Don't you love that! I do, but this morning as Luci was reading over these first six chapters, she said to me, "Now, Marilyn, I'm not positive I know what the word *non sequitur* means. I'm fairly certain I know its meaning by the way you're using it, but just to be clear, would you mind defining it for me?"

I felt that was totally reasonable. Because we're writing this book together, she needs to know if my words might get us both in trouble. So, wanting to be on the safe side, I gave her the dictionary definition of *non sequitur*. It's "a statement that does not follow logically from what preceded it."

Then, for the sake of overkill, I gave her an example of two imaginary characters (for simplicity's sake, we'll call them Marilyn and Luci) having a completely non sequitur conversation:

Luci: "I brought my purse in here. Have you seen it?"

Marilyn: "These pants are new. Do you think they make my butt look big?"

Luci: "I cannot believe we go on water rationing next month. My flowers will die."

Marilyn: "Why would anyone want a dog when a cat is so much less demanding?"

Luci: "Well, finally here's an ice cream with no sugar, no carbs, and no artificial flavors. It's called Bluh."

Marilyn: "Why is that woman standing in the middle of my driveway screaming that non sequiturs give her a stomachache?"

Having completed the overkill illustration, I asked Luci if I'd made the meaning of non sequiturs understandable. "Yes you have, honey," she answered, "and just for the record, I'm the one in the driveway screaming."

DEFYING DEFEAT AND CHOOSING VICTORY

Now it's time to get back to work. We've been talking about what we're made of and wondering how strong and courageous we would be if our life circumstances took a sudden and disastrous left turn. How would we behave? Would we defy defeat and choose victory? Would we have the right stuff? While we acknowledge that DNA or our environment—or both—play a role in determining our physical makeup as well as our character, we've agreed (I hope) that an even bigger part of any survival explanation has got to be the sovereign hand of God.

There is comfort in recognizing God's role in our having the right stuff. In short, our lives are *meant* to work. He has given us what it takes to survive any challenges that confront us. He has equipped us (through our DNA and environment) for survival. But the degree to which we utilize that equipping (through good choices and obedient responses to the divine blueprint) is up to us.

We can survive a bad environment, and we can survive weak DNA. Our challenge is to be obedient to what God has called us to do with the skills we've been given to do it.

For example, I have neither the DNA nor the inherent skills to understand physics. My environment did not work against that science. I am simply missing the "physics gene," assuming there is one. That being the case, God did not ordain for me to work in the space program designing nuclear equipment for rocket launches. He knew that would be a mistake, possibly with huge global ramifications.

In all our life experiences, it is He who provides our "stuff," even though human elements contribute as well. Sometimes we are not even aware of how much "right stuff" we have until we face the challenges of adversity.

QUEEN ESTHER: A MELDING OF SOVEREIGNTY AND STUFF

Esther is one of my favorite Bible characters, and the book of Esther is one of my favorite parts of the Old Testament. Esther was a perfect melding of stuff and sovereignty. I'll refresh your memory on the details of her life and how God put her in a position to defy defeat and choose victory—not only for herself but for the millions of other Jews living in Persia at that time.

Esther was a little orphan girl who had been adopted by her relative Mordecai to nurture and to raise. Mordecai was known to be a devout Jew: righteous, godly, and highly respected by all who knew him. Esther grew to be a beautiful young woman who was picked to be the new queen of King Xerxes, the ruler of 127 provinces that stretched from India to Ethiopia. He was the most powerful man in the world during the time of his reign. He had fallen in love with Esther's dignity, beauty, and grace, and he was proud to share his throne with such a stunningly gorgeous woman.

All was well in the kingdom until a Jew-hating man named Haman devised a plot to kill all the Jews in Persia. Haman, who held a place of influential authority in the king's court, despised Mordecai because he would not bow down in honor and respect to Haman. Haman also despised Mordecai's Jewishness.

When Mordecai heard of Haman's plot to have the Jews destroyed, he went to Esther and urged her to use the position God in His sovereignty had designed for her, as rescuer of her people. She agreed to speak to the king on behalf of the Jews, even though she would do it at great risk to her own life. Esther said to Mordecai, "All the king's officials and the people of the royal provinces know that for any man or woman who approaches the king in the inner court without being summoned the king has but one law: that he be put to death" (4:11).

Despite the danger, Esther agreed to approach the king even though it was against the law, telling Mordecai, "If I perish, I perish" (v. 16).

What was Haman's plot, and why did King Xerxes agree to it? In Esther 3:8–11 we read how Haman laid it out for the king—and how the king responded.

> Then Haman said to King Xerxes, "There is a certain people dispersed and scattered among the peoples in all the provinces of your kingdom whose customs are different from those of all other people and who do not obey the king's laws; it is not in the king's best interest to tolerate them. If it pleases the king, let a decree be issued to destroy them."
>
> The king said to Haman, " Do with the people as you please."

King Xerxes was basically unaware of the Jews in his kingdom and completely disinterested in their future. When Haman appealed to the king's vanity by saying the Jews did not obey the king's laws, Xerxes apparently found that reason enough to get rid of them. But Xerxes did not know his beloved wife was a Jew! So he did not know his decree would mean that she and all the people of her faith would be killed.

When Mordecai heard what had happened, he urged Esther to speak up for her people. His words, recorded in Esther 4:14, are memorable: "Who knows but that you have come to royal position for such a time as this?"

When Esther bravely told the king that his decree would mean her death and the annihilation of her people, he was furious. King Xerxes had Haman hung on the gallows Haman had prepared for Mordecai. The Jewish people were saved from mass destruction by the brave and timely courage of a Jewish queen who risked her life to plead with the king for her people.

CALLED AND EQUIPPED

As we consider Esther's sovereignly designed position at that point in history, we see clearly the order in God's blueprint. In His time His will is accomplished. God first equipped Esther for the task by creating her as a beautiful woman, inside and out, who was sure to win the heart of the king. She was winsome and humble, reflecting the spirit of the home in which she had been reared by Mordecai. She was also selfless and bold: she chose to risk her life and live out her faith rather than hide her Jewishness from the king and, perhaps, survive the purge. By her act, the "stuff" she was made of became apparent to her and to those around her.

Prior to taking a stand against Haman and for her people, Esther was an indulged, privileged, and deeply loved queen. Life was easy. Why rock the boat? But that's just what she did. She heeded Mordecai's words and proved that she was, indeed, divinely chosen for "such a time as this." Her courage won liberty and freedom to God's people. That act was her divine destiny.

What about *our* divine destiny? Do we have the "stuff" to accomplish it? Absolutely! I don't know who said this, but I believe it: "Whom He calls He also equips." I believe we all have been called to share the good news of freedom through salvation. We've been called to proclaim the message that will "free the captives from prison" (Isaiah 42:7 NLT). That gospel-message is reinforced in the life of Jesus Christ. We may be secure and anonymous right now, as Esther was. But the day will come for all of us when we hear these words in the forefront of our minds: *I was born for such a time as this.*

God's will is accomplished as He enables us to rise to the challenges that confront us. He equips us as surely as He calls us.

AFTERTHOUGHT

"Marilyn, I am still bothered by the word *non sequitur*."

"Don't you mean, Luci, you are bothered by the fact of non sequiturs because they give you a stomachache?"

"That is not it at all, Marilyn. I can take a Pepcid AC

for what non sequiturs do to my system. I am bothered by the word. Actually, it seems to me non sequitur is two words, which would make it a phrase instead of a word. Apparently sequitur is not a word by itself. *Non* means "not," so why is there not a sequitur that is a word by itself? You know this sort of thing threatens my need for order. Help me, Marilyn . . . I'm nauseous."

"I think, Luci, you will find the gingham fabric goes perfectly with your new blue purse. I strongly recommend you pack it for your next trip."

5

Loving Others Unconditionally

Loving even those whose behavior is unacceptable

Mark Twain said, "Always acknowledge a fault frankly. This will throw those in authority off their guard and give you an opportunity to commit more." It is true that we get a bit whiplashed when a fault is frankly acknowledged, perhaps because it's such a rare thing to encounter. Generally people come up with multiple excuses and rationalizations before ever admitting to a fault.

I remember confronting our then-five-year-old son, Jeff, with the fact that I knew he was taking money out of my purse. When I first discovered his thievery I was shocked. Visions of future jail sentences filled my mind. My heart sank as I scrambled to determine where I was failing and how he had missed knowing the simple commandment "Thou shalt not steal." I also wondered why he only took pennies. If he was going to be a thief, why not go for bigger booty?

On the morning I chose to have my heart-to-heart chat with Jeff, I was prepared not only to confront him with his moral and ethical turpitude, but to tell him I had actually seen him rummaging through my coin purse. With that kind of convincing evidence, he would have no choice but admit his fault because I was an eye-witness.

When I gathered him up on my lap and asked him why he was taking pennies out of my purse, he replied without hesitation that he needed the money. I asked him what he needed the money for, and again his response came quickly: he said he liked the sound the pennies made in his pocket. Apparently Jeff and Tommy Turner were swaggering around the neighborhood with jingling pockets.

I had expected at least a little resistance from Jeff when I asked for an explanation about the stolen pennies. Since he provided none, as Twain predicted, I was thrown off guard. Jeff assured me he would not be stealing any more pennies, so I felt there was at least hope for his little thieving soul. But he told me the reason he did not need more pennies was because his pockets were now full. And he added that since he did not need more pennies, I could quit spying on him.

LOVING OTHERS AS GOD LOVES US

Perhaps you know that I was once a teacher of college students. Although I've moved on to other pursuits, the teacher tendencies in me sometimes re-exert themselves, and now is one of those times. So, let's take a moment to review: The premise of this book is that Christ's loving gift of salvation gives us amazing freedom, inside and out. My hope is that in these first chapters, I have shown you how to know who you really are, as God knows you. I've reminded you that He loves you no matter what you find when you delve into your innermost thoughts and feelings. In acknowledging and valuing His constant, unwavering love, you can find freedom from the hard and hurtful experiences of life, and you can get beyond even those old, painful wounds that refuse to heal.

God created us, and He has a plan for us, a plan that leads to our divine destiny. He has put within us the "right stuff" that can, if we choose to utilize it, enable us to defy defeat and accomplish that destiny. He has equipped us to choose victory when adversity strikes.

Knowing we have what it takes, we're freed from living in fear that bad "somethings" might happen to us in the future. Something bad probably *will* happen, but we'll get through it, with God's help.

What a wonderfully amazing gift God has given us: freedom that comes from knowing and loving our authentic self, freedom that takes us beyond our past hurts and still-bleeding wounds, and freedom from the fear of what lies in the future. Such a gift is really too good to keep solely for our exclusive use, don't you think? (Although I've acknowledged my occasional preference for selfishness, especially about such things as patio furniture, when it comes to sharing anything related to the love of Christ and His gospel message, I'm completely relieved of my self-centeredness and eager to pass along the bountiful blessings I've been given.)

As believers, we know we're loved by a compassionate God, and we're taught by His Word to love ourselves as Christ loves us, unconditionally. We may have behaviors that require determined work in order to be changed, but we are to love ourselves despite our shortcomings because that's how Christ loves us.

Once we accept and understand the extraordinary love Jesus has for us, we're ready to take the next step: sharing that same unconditional love with others. Jesus told His followers (including you and me today), "Love your neighbor as yourself" (Matthew 19:19). That directive is repeated several times in the New Testament (see, for example, Matthew 22:39; Mark 12:31, 33; Romans 13:8–9). It's so important, in fact, that Jesus described it as the second-greatest commandment:

> "You shall love the LORD your God with all your heart, with all your soul, and with all your mind." This is the first and great commandment. And the second is like it: "You shall love your neighbor as yourself." On these two commandments hang all the Law and the Prophets. (Matthew 22:37–40 NKJV)

When an "expert in the law" asked Jesus, "And who is my neighbor?" Jesus replied by telling a parable describing a traveler waylaid by thieves who "stripped him of his clothes, beat him and went away, leaving him half dead" (Luke 10:30). Good-guy passersby—a priest and a Levite (probably wearing white hats)—who would have been expected to help the poor traveler did not bother to do so. But a bad-guy Samaritan (wearing a black turban, no doubt), someone who would not have been expected to help a Jew, given the mutual disdain the two groups held for each other, rendered compassionate aid and generously sought help for him.

"Which of these three do you think was a neighbor to the man who fell into the hands of robbers?" Jesus asked the expert.

"The one who had mercy on him," the expert correctly answered (see Luke 10:25–37).

We're to love our neighbors, and that means everybody, including unlikable characters with whom we'd prefer not to associate, wounded and waylaid persons we'd rather pass by on the other side of the road, and assorted other misfits who are just as imperfect as we are. It's hard to accept sometimes, but it's what Jesus wants us to do: accept others as they are, in the same way He accepts us, with all our flaws and failures.

JUST HOW MUCH DO WE HAVE TO ACCEPT?

When we consider the broad topic of accepting people as they are, we naturally wonder, *But just how much do we accept?* Is it wise to extend a blanket acceptance with no dialogue about a few things that may be troublesome? And if we only "accept" one another, don't those unspoken things loom up like barricades that prevent authentic intimacy? Finally, aren't there limits to be placed on acceptance?

In regard to my son, Jeff, I owed him, as a mother, the teaching that some behavior is not acceptable. I needed to teach him that stealing is wrong. It is not acceptable to God, and neither is it acceptable to Mama. Of course, at the same time, I separated his behavior from his worth as a child. I needed to show Jeff my love for him as my darling little boy, even though he might one day be heading for the penitentiary if he did not change his ways. (I did not threaten him with the penitentiary. I was only amusing myself as I wrote that sentence.)

My *total acceptance* of Jeff is based on my *total love* for him. His behavior does not diminish my love. That is as true for this mother-heart now at his present age of forty-two as it was when he was five. It is the same way my Father God loves me at my present age of . . . well, at my present age. But within that love, troublesome behavior needs to be dealt with. This is true in all relationships, not just the mother-child relationship. So to answer the question, are there limits to acceptance? yes, I believe there are.

But if there are limits to acceptance, does that mean my love is not unconditional? Does that mean I'll love you unless you do something I don't like? If you annoy me, physically hurt me, betray me, or abuse me so that our relationship is strained to the breaking point, do I have the right to say, "I'm outta here"?

I do believe there are breaking points in a relationship, and when one of those breaking points occurs, it may no longer be advisable to stick around. *Acceptance* is not the same as *love*, so limiting one's acceptance of someone is not the same as loving with conditions. I may ultimately need to put distance between myself and someone whose behavior is unacceptable to me. That distance does not have to mean I no longer love that person unconditionally. It may simply mean it is not healthy for me to be in close proximity to him or her. It is possible to love the person but refuse his or her behavior. It is also possible to love that person but never see him or her again.

Why would such a thing happen? Because the person's behavior is toxic to me, and toxicity is bad for my health. In fact, toxicity can be deadly. I am responsible to myself to take care of myself.

Let's refresh our minds on the meaning of the phrase *unconditional love*. We know the word *conditional* means "to place or impose conditions." The prefix *un* means "not"; therefore, *unconditional* means "not placing conditions." So then, how can we say we love unconditionally if someone's behavior is toxic and we leave to protect ourselves? Am I not placing conditions if I cannot accept how he or she is behaving? Yes, I am. But those conditions do not have to negate my love. They do, however, dictate my response to that person when his or her behaviors are toxic. Unconditional love means I don't refuse that person a place in my heart. But I may refuse him or her a place in my home or my life. It may mean loving from a distance.

Let's swing back to my little boy, Jeff. If he continued going through my purse and taking money from me, his behavior would need to continually be addressed by me. If he grew up and learned how to get money out of my bank account and periodically drained that account as he chose, I would then do more than simply "address" the issue. He would need to know I might be forced to take legal action. If, when he visited me, I found little things missing after he left, I would ultimately not allow him to visit in my home. Because his behavior would be unacceptable to me.

Would I still love him unconditionally? Yes. I would love his heart that needs redeeming. I would love him for the soul God created but a soul who made poor choices that caused my mother-heart to become suspicious and no longer trusting. I would love him unconditionally until the day I die. But my love would circle around his behavior and love him in spite of it. I wouldn't accept his behavior, and I would not feel guilty about my refusal to accept it. But at the same time, I would love him with a love I can't turn off.

Now, may I emphasize this fact in case my illustration of Jeff is misleading: Jeff did not grow up to be a thief. He has never drained my bank account. He has never left my home with things he decided to scoop up and take with him. Jeff is a perfect son, a perfect citizen, and a perfect Christian. (Ahem!) But if he were not . . . I'd love him anyway!

In our imperfect world, the reality is that some people

are toxic, and we are justified in not wanting them in our life. But refusing someone access to us does not mean we don't love that person unconditionally. It means we are choosing to avoid the toxicity he or she brings into our life as a result of unacceptable behavior. We want to remember it is possible for us to love at a distance; in fact, it's sometimes preferable.

LIMITS ON ACCEPTANCE

There are, indeed, limits to how much we accept of others, and each of us needs to know what those limits are. In the next chapter, we'll discuss how we set those boundaries. In the remainder of this chapter, I'd like to discuss how we can recognize behaviors that *always* exceed the limits and what we can do when such situations occur, and also how we can handle behavior that is irritating but probably not dangerous.

I received a letter from a woman this week detailing the sexually abusive behavior of her alcoholic husband. She said she thought she had reached her limit but felt afraid to leave because she has no job skills and three young children. She fears she will not be able to financially take care of them.

We don't all have the same limits on the behaviors we will accept in others. What I could manage to accept might be less than you decide you could handle. But there are certain behaviors that should go beyond the limits of what is acceptable for any of us. When this woman became aware that her husband was sexually fondling their eight-year-old daughter, she was understandably horrified. In my view, he had passed the limits that apply to everyone. There is no way his behavior can be excused or tolerated; it is totally unacceptable.

But what does she do if she has no job skills, no money, and no place to go? The one thing she cannot do is do nothing. What are her options? Admittedly, they are few. Others in her situation might need to find temporary housing in a women's shelter or seek help from law-enforcement officials. Fortunately, she has a loving mother who has offered to have the woman and her children move in with her as long as they need to.

Granted, moving in with extended family may not be an ideal situation, but this little eight-year-old girl is emotionally hurt and in need of compassionate love, care, and empathy. She needs to feel safe from a continuation of this abuse, and she needs to see a professional who can walk her through steps that will, hopefully, lead to healing. If the mother chose not to leave, the sexual behavior of the father would undoubtedly continue, resulting in even deeper emotional and sexual victimization of the child. That is totally unacceptable.

The same is true for physical abuse. The woman who

wrote to me, and her children, are experiencing this kind of abuse when her husband flies into his alcoholic rages. Just for discussion purposes, let's suppose there's no sexual abuse going on and the behavior is "only" physical. What should her limit be then? Does she stay if he only rages once a week? Does she stay as long as there are no broken bones? Does she stay if he ultimately shows remorse and begs her not to leave? If he promises never to take another drink and never to hurt her and the children again, does she stay?

Is there any way to say his behavior is acceptable? No. There is no way. In my opinion, physical abuse is totally unacceptable.

The facts are that this woman's children have been put in physical, emotional, and sexual jeopardy, and she has a God-given responsibility to protect them. Therefore, I would counsel her to leave. If he enters into treatment for his unacceptable behaviors (in this case, alcoholism as well as committing sexual and physical abuse), there may be hope for recovery if he makes the decision to get it. But until then . . .

I am dogmatic about condemning any behavior that victimizes a child; the safety of the child must always be the number one priority of all caregivers. A child is completely dependent upon the caregiver, and it is totally unacceptable to put a child at sexual, physical, or emotional risk. Children cannot care for themselves; for that reason, the adult world must accept full responsibility for all aspects of their lives.

Jesus was very clear about how children are to be thought of and treated. In Matthew 18, when the disciples sank to an unattractive low and asked Jesus, "Which of us is greatest in the Kingdom of Heaven?" Jesus told them a child would be greatest (vv. 1–3 NLT). The reason? The child's humble innocence. Jesus then stated a warning concerning the treatment of a child: "If anyone causes one of these little ones who trusts in me to lose faith, it would be better for that person to be thrown into the sea with a large millstone tied around the neck" (v. 6 NLT).

A parent or caretaker who does not provide for the safety of a child is creating in the child a distrust of adults and often, a distrust of God. Jesus does not find it acceptable when a child's faith is destroyed; neither should we.

ANNOYING, UNATTRACTIVE, OR UNACCEPTABLE BEHAVIORS

The behaviors we've just discussed are huge issues that threaten children and destroy the safety of the home. We've agreed those behaviors are unacceptable. But what about behavior that is simply an annoyance? No one is threatened or harmed by it . . . just annoyed, perhaps to the point of going stir-crazy.

For example, Bernadette Petfarken has the annoying habit of constantly interrupting when I'm talking. Rarely is it possible for me to finish a sentence before she breaks in with her own thoughts, which may have nothing to do with what I am saying. (She is the queen of conversational non sequiturs.)

Is Bernadette's behavior acceptable? To me it is not, but I have to decide the degree to which it is not. In other words, does that habit annoy me to the point I want to drop Bernadette from the list of my current friends and potential pallbearers? Shall I distance myself completely from her as I would from someone whose behavior is unacceptable? Or does she have other redeeming qualities that are sufficiently positive that cause me to overlook the nonlistening, constantly interrupting, and apparently disinterested habit she has perfected?

I have a choice: Do I move Bernadette to my former-friends category and avoid her completely? Do I limit my exposure to her to brief encounters in which I hold no expectation of speaking without interruption? Or do I continue in our current relationship but buy a mouth guard to protect my molars from being ground into powder as I seethe in annoyance at Bernadette's infernal interrupting?

Of course, there is another alternative I might

choose, and it is the ideal solution for my difficulty with Bernadette's behavior: she and I could have a nonthreatening chat in which I tell her how much I care about our relationship. I could say, honestly and gently, with quiet compassion and spiritual maturity, that her interruptions inspire murderous impulses in me, which I fear one day I may act upon! (Once again, don't take the murder part seriously; I'm only amusing myself.)

Either that, or I might say, "Sweet baby, I value your friendship and adore the way you snort when you laugh. But I would enjoy our conversations so much more if you would please listen while I am expounding on some brilliant thought and not interrupt until I manage to complete it, and I do promise to work on speaking more succinctly in the future so that you can get on with what *you* are eager to say."

The fact is, talking with each other candidly, in a nonthreatening way, is the ideal solution for addressing all behaviors we find unacceptable. Granted, in situations where addiction, violence, and/or sexual abuse is occurring, legal intervention and professional help may be necessary to stop the addiction or abuse and bring about healing. But communicating our thoughts and feelings to one another is crucial to the health of our relationships, and in most cases it is the first step toward naming and eliminating unacceptable behavior. To do that we need to use words.

Perhaps that is one explanation for my evolving from being a college instructor of English and literature to becoming a trained mental-health professional providing help to those in need of therapy. Through God's mercy and with the compassion and love extended by friends and professionals, I have endured some difficult life storms: the death of a child and the death of a husband, to name just two. More recently, I've survived a debilitating illness, and I've also struggled with the same challenging family issues millions of others have had to endure.

Having been the recipient of loving help and compassionate understanding during my own difficulties, I longed to pass on those gifts to others in need. At the same time, I have always loved to study, practice, and teach effective communication. Blending those two passions, I completed my master's degree in counseling psychology and spent many years helping persons learn to accurately identify their authentic feelings and then express them aloud to themselves, to me, and, if appropriate, to others.

I've seen how open and honest communication can establish self-worth and restore damaged relationships. I do love words! So I especially love Proverbs 18:20:

Words satisfy the soul as food satisfies the stomach;
the right words on a person's lips bring satisfaction.
(NLT)

My peace-loving friend Luci also loves words, and she is extremely comfortable and skilled in using them. She is a delight to listen to and a pleasure to read. I consider her a master of words who has no peers, unless it might possibly be her baby brother, Chuck. Word mastery seems to run in the Swindoll family. But there is one word area from which Luci retreats, one situation in which she is noticeably uncomfortable. Whereas I would happily sit down with you and discuss how modifying your annoying or unacceptable behaviors could strengthen our relationship, Luci hates to confront anyone about anything. She has told me repeatedly she wants people to just know that what they are doing is unacceptable or annoying and then change what they're doing. When I tell Luci she will feel better if she says something and clears up the problem, she declines. She would rather put up with the annoying behavior than address it.

This brings up an unacceptable behavior I find in myself: I am never hesitant to give my opinion on anything. I can enthusiastically share my thoughts on any subject anywhere at any time and only later realize no one asked for my opinion. Too late, I realize I should have "rested my voice."

Now, as I write those words, the little voice living in me who wants to protect my public image says, "Marilyn, maybe it would be more accurate if you just said your forthright use of words can be an unattractive trait. Don't you think throwing that characteristic into the unacceptable pile is a bit harsh?"

Well, maybe, especially compared with the "totally unacceptable" behaviors (such as sexual and physical abuse) mentioned earlier. But here's why I'll stick with my decision to put my spouting off of unsolicited opinions in the unacceptable category. It's a given that anything unacceptable is already unattractive. How it went from unattractive to unacceptable has to do with limits, which vary from person to person. What might be simply unattractive to some is unacceptable to others. I think in all fairness to my desire to grow into a more agreeable and pleasant little old lady, I need to accept that my overly free use of words is, for me, unacceptable. This is a serious personal consideration, because if I am unacceptable, who am I going to tell my opinions to?

GOD'S UNFATHOMABLE LOVE

Although it is the goal toward which we strive, if the truth were known, not one of us is able to fully accept others. None of us is able to fully accept ourselves either. We know too much. We see others and ourselves in the light of reality, and sometimes we tend to step back from that reality. It isn't always to our liking; it isn't always a pretty picture.

That's why God's love for us is difficult to grasp. He knows what we know. In fact, He knows even more. Yet there it is: His unconditional love. It's interesting He does not circle around us to keep from encountering our weaknesses and imperfections. Why? Because once they are confessed and forgiven He takes no notice of them. Scripture says He does not even remember them. "Their sins and lawless acts I will remember no more," He says in Hebrews 10:17.

Can you imagine greater freedom for our guilt-prone souls than to fully realize He does not remember our sins? And, in turn, can you imagine the gift we give others when we extend that kind of unconditional love to them? While my son, Jeff, has lived a life that has kept him free from the threat of ever hearing a penitentiary cell door slam shut behind him, there are many sons and daughters—parents and siblings too—who are there today. Their behavior has been unacceptable to others, as well as to society as a whole, and they are living out the consequences of that behavior. Others are not imprisoned physically but exhibit behaviors that are unacceptable for those who otherwise might want to live or associate with them.

But out there too are sons and daughters, parents and siblings, who, while undoubtedly disapproving of the unacceptable behavior, continue to love those persons anyway, despite their flaws. They may have to love from a distance, but theirs is a love that won't let go. It is the same love with which our Father encloses us.

6

Setting Boundaries
When You'd Rather Not

Dealing with those who want more than you can or want to give

When I first moved into my Frisco home, I was charmed by my neighbor Paula's two little dogs. When either or both of them burst through their doggie door into the backyard, they bark ferociously at whatever got their attention and forced them to no longer languish about the house. To my knowledge, nothing has occurred in the neighborhood that warrants their furious barking, but perhaps that's because the violators have been frightened away.

What gives me a giggle is how easily these two little

fur balls can be talked out of being ferocious warriors. When I walk into my backyard they somehow know it and come leaping out of their house, ever ready to defend their property should I be inclined to climb the fence. All I have to do to remind them I am their new and favorite neighbor is hunch down and talk baby talk to them. Then they both duck their heads and wag their tails. Each seems embarrassed they forgot what a "wufuly and pwecious wady" I am. They're also responsive to being reminded they are "butiful and wuvable."

But something else attracted my studied attention to these two little characters. When I first moved in, I noticed how amazingly conscientious they were to not get into the flower beds that flanked their mistress's backyard. Whatever their duties, all business was conducted in the grassy area. I couldn't help compare them to the dogs who live with my son, Jeff, and his wife, Carla; those dogs find flower beds irresistible. They lie in them, roll in them, and on occasion feel compelled to dig up flowers and relocate them. Paula's dogs showed no such uncivilized inclinations.

One morning when Paula and I were simultaneously watering our backyard plants, I told her how impressed I was that her dogs stayed out of the flower beds. She laughed and explained that an invisible, electronic fence circles the beds. Should the dogs stray into them, they would experience a little shock from their electronically programmed dog collars. As a result, neither shows the slightest interest in the petunias.

I momentarily pondered wearing an electronic collar to prevent my straying into "chocolate beds," but quickly dismissed the thought.

It may seem odd to consider an electronic fence as an agent of freedom, but the result of observing the boundary between grass and flowers keeps the dogs out of trouble. They aren't scolded or exiled to the garage for bad behavior. Instead they have the freedom to bark at all interesting persons and the peace of knowing they are not upsetting Mama by messing up her flowers.

Might that not be true for those of us who are not in the dog world but who need fencing encouragement? Knowing what those fences or boundaries are keeps us from guessing—and as a result keeps us out of trouble with Mama and "whombody else." (I got that phrase from the late Victor Borge. If you remember his comedic performances, you and I were in high school in the late fifties.)

THE BENEFIT OF BOUNDARIES

As we talk about boundaries in this chapter and how they provide us with freedom (perhaps contrary to what one would at first assume a boundary would do), we need to first establish a working definition of just what a *boundary* is. The dictionary defines it as "something that indicates a border or limit." That's the kind of boundary Paula needed to set for her dogs. It's a great visual aid for us as we think about necessary boundaries. But as we use the word *boundary* here in the context of how it creates "inside freedom," we narrow its meaning to one that has to do with limiting human behavior more than as an observance of geographical or property borders.

I suppose in the days of the Old West the need for a behavioral boundary was communicated by the cowboy drawing a line in the dirt with the toe of his boot and saying, "Ya go over that line, and I'll shoot ya dead." We've always been aware of the need for boundaries on certain behaviors, but there are better ways of establishing them than with a six-shooter.

For example, in the previous chapter on loving others unconditionally, the woman who wrote to me about her sexually and physically abusive husband needed to establish clear boundaries with him. He had to know if he continued to cross the line there would be consequences to his choice. The first consequence would be her refusal to allow his behavior to continue, and if it did, the next consequence would be that she would take the children and leave.

One of the necessary components to establishing a

boundary is that it must be clearly stated as well as clearly understood. The consequence for not honoring the boundary does not necessarily need to be stated in the beginning when the boundary is set. For example, when little Augusta wants to eat a brownie ten minutes before dinner, Mama states the boundary: no brownie before dinner. When Augusta grabs a brownie, stuffs it in her mouth, and then rushes to the bathroom so she can chew in privacy, it is time then for Augusta to know the consequence.

But what if Mama pretends she did not see Augusta grab and flee? Augusta learns that Mama does not always mean what she says and that sometimes she can ignore the boundary and get by with it. Augusta needs to know what the boundary is and that it will always be enforced. That consistency provides security for Augusta, who learns as a child that a boundary is to be honored—and that she too may have boundaries that must be honored as well.

As the result of blurred boundaries during childhood, many of us have never fully known we are entitled to *have* boundaries. What does the behavior of someone who has blurred boundaries look like? One of those behaviors is the inability to say no. The word *no* is a great communicator of a clear boundary. But many persons do not feel they are entitled to say no. They assume the best way to get along in life and be valued is to be agreeable. Saying no is not being agreeable and might even make someone mad. Also, saying no may make us appear to be selfish and concerned only about things that give us personal satisfaction. By saying no we may appear to be putting our needs ahead of the needs of others. That, we assume, is clearly selfish. But such is not always the case.

Let's use Althea as an example of one who can say no and not feel she is being selfish in using the word. She was asked to be the group leader for seventy-five women from her church who were attending a Women of Faith conference. The conference was in a city several hours away from the church community and would require bus transportation. The job of arranging transportation, hotel, food, ticketing, and general well-being for all the members of the group was a huge responsibility, one Althea knew well because she had accepted the job the previous year, and it had proven to be an enormous energy drain for her.

So when she was asked to take on the job a second time, she said no to the women's ministry chairperson. She did so firmly but pleasantly so there was no misunderstanding, justifying her *no* by simply stating that this year she wanted to drive her own car to the conference with two friends and then sit back and enjoy it free from organizational responsibility. Althea did not feel she was being selfish. And I agree.

BOUNDARIES FOR SELF-PRESERVATION

We are taught by Jesus's example to have the heart of a servant; He told the disciples, "I am among you as the One who serves" (Luke 22:27 NKJV). But have you ever wondered, *If we are on this earth to serve the needs of others, what are those others doing?*

In Althea's case, she served the needs of her church group; the next year, however, she joined the "others" group. Quite frankly, I think being in the "others" group from time to time is healthy and that using the unmistakably clear boundary word *no* can be a fair and mutually beneficial choice. It is true we are called to love as Jesus loves and to serve others in love, as He did. But that does not mean we don't take care of ourselves as we do so.

Again we learn from Jesus's example. Mark 3:9–10 describes a time when Jesus got in a boat to get away from the pressing crowd. He did this not to escape their need but to preserve Himself. He knew His earthly body needed protection from the pressure and prodding of all those anxious people, so He spoke to them from a boat.

We are not told that He specifically said no to anyone in the crowd who wanted His help, but by reading Mark's account of what happened, we can perceive that His actions were saying no for Him. Being separated from the crowd meant there were many who could not touch Him and be healed of their illnesses. In effect, he was telling them no.

Was Jesus being selfish? Hardly. His behavior is an example of the right for self-preservation. Often the word *no*, spoken aloud or expressed clearly through our actions, is necessary for our well-being.

Sometimes boundaries protect us from overextending ourselves to others, and sometimes they protect us from the ill effects that result from our own desires and habits. For instance, although we know a potentially dangerous or harmful indulgence of some sort might bring momentary pleasure, we establish a boundary that keeps us from that indulgence. Behind that boundary, we enjoy freedom from addiction or the freedom of good health unmarred by the damages the indulgence might bring.

Similarly, boundaries create freedom within relationships. The wedding vows, for example, are intended to free us from our worries of infidelity and jealousy. By exchanging these vows, two spouses set mutually agreed-upon boundaries, and within those boundaries, love, happiness, and harmony are shared. If, on the other hand, the boundaries are violated, hard consequences may result.

Even between friends, boundaries are freeing. For example, Luci hates to have anyone eat off her plate. We have agreed that I will never reach over with my fork to assist her in finishing her pie. I think that is a totally reasonable boundary, and I have observed it carefully ever since her fork left marks on my right hand.

BOUNDARIES OF SELF-DEFENSE

Saying no is not only a strong, clear way to act for our self-preservation; it's also a good self-defense word. Looking back to the little brownie-snatching Augusta, if she learned from her mother that no meant no, she might be more fully prepared to give a no response when her uncle tried to touch her inappropriately. She could respond to him with strength and opposition, having been taught that some behaviors are not acceptable and need to be resisted.

My grandson Alec looks like a hunky football player you don't want to be tackled by. He is truly a formidable-appearing nine-year-old boy. Here's the essence of the conversation we had several nights ago when we were talking on the phone:

> "Maungya, yesterday I had to coldcock Jamie Hatcher."
>
> "You had to *what*?"
>
> "I had to coldcock Jamie."
>
> "Well, honey, what in the world does that *coldcock* word mean?"

"It means I had to punch him in the neck."

"Mercy, Alec! That sounds violent. Why did you have to do that?"

"'Cause, Maungya, sometimes that's what ya gotta do if a guy won't take no for an answer."

I got the point. When saying no doesn't work, sometimes we have to "say" it another way. Maybe the cold-cock has replaced the six-shooter.

OUR AWESOME FREEDOM OF CHOICE

I believe the most interesting *no* boundary was initiated by God. Paradoxically, that no is intended to provide us with freedom of choice. We can choose freedom, or we can choose to become enslaved. It all depends on how we use our freedom of choice.

Let's do a giggle break here, but this time the joke is not a non sequitur.

One day God was looking down at earth and saw the result of the outrageously bad choices His creation was making. He decided to send down an angel to do a little research.

When the angel returned, he reported that 95 percent of the people were behaving badly and 5 percent were not. God was not pleased, so He decided to e-mail the 5 percent who were behaving well and commend them for their good choices.

Do you know what that e-mail said?

Just wondering, because I didn't get one either.

When you've regained your composure after all that giggling, let me point out that the reality is, more people do make good choices than bad. If that were not so, the world would be even more chaotic than it is.

How awesome it is to realize God chose to give all creation the option to make personal choices based on personal preferences. When He settled Adam and Eve in the Garden of Eden, He invited them to enjoy everything there . . . except for one tree. Around that tree God drew a boundary; He pointed to that tree and said no.

Why did God put the tree in the Garden if they weren't allowed to eat its fruit? To give them a choice. They could choose to obey or to disobey. When Satan showed up and encouraged Eve to eat of the tree of the knowledge of good and evil, she made her choice. She disobeyed God. Then her witless husband joined her in her choice of disobedience. As a result, the consequence of sin hurled itself upon the world. Order and perfection were lost in an instant by this sin choice. The comfort and luxury of perfection were no longer available in Eden or anywhere else in the world. From that point on, all creation has struggled for goodness, order, and peace.

The centuries-old question of why God allowed such

disastrous choices is a fair one. Could God not have prevented Adam and Eve from disobeying Him? Could He not have said, "You are not allowed to disobey Me," and that would have been the end of it? Of course He could. Instead, God allowed creation to choose its own boundary. If He had prevented Adam and Eve's disobedience, He would not have honored the boundary they chose, the boundary that allowed them . . . and allows us . . . to say no to God: no, God, we will not always obey You.

Where there is no freedom of choice there is a dictatorship. God chose against divine tyranny. His desire is that we choose to love Him. But we are not little programmed automatons who are being good and doing good because there is no other choice. There *is* a choice.

God's choice for us is that we would respond to His offer of love. But each one of us can choose. We can accept that offer, or we can say no to it. So many times throughout history, that is exactly what God's creation has done. I find one of the most poignant passages in Scripture is the image of Jesus described in Matthew 23:37. Gazing down upon His city, He says,

O Jerusalem, Jerusalem, the one who kills the prophets and stones those who are sent to her! How often I wanted to gather your children together, as a hen gathers her chicks under her wings, but you were not willing!

Like Jerusalem of old, we have the option to exercise our *no* boundary. We can choose to tell God not to cross the line we've drawn to keep Him out of our life, and He will honor that choice—but at great cost to our soul's freedom. As the poet said, "Many of us are wandering lost upon the mountains of our choice."

Authentic freedom comes when we choose to crawl under the canopy created by the wings of God's love and live within His protective boundaries. He says to us, "Come to me, . . . and I will give you rest" (Matthew 11:28). In Him we find both respite . . . and freedom.

PART 2

Free on the Outside

Luci Swindoll

7

Giving Because You've Been Given To

*Getting beyond the bondage of debt and
learning to give the way God gives to us*

In January 2001 the core speaking team of Women of
Faith had an opportunity to meet Dr. Os Guinness. He
was invited to spend a day with us, and to speak about
anything on his mind. He chose the topic of freedom,
and I will never forget that day or what he said. It made
a lasting impression on me.

Os was born in China of missionary parents during
World War II. Before he turned five, there was a famine
in the area where his family was living, and millions
died, including his two brothers. The first ten years of

his life he lived in a Buddhist culture. He was educated in England, is a graduate of Oxford University, and has traveled the world. He came to faith in Jesus Christ in the late 1960s, a time when everything about Christendom was being challenged. Os brings with him an unshakable security about the truth of the Bible and a sense of extraordinary relevance regarding faith for practical living. He is ever seeking to know God more personally and deeply. It was out of this seedbed of thought and living that he spoke to our group, and we hung on every word.

Near the end of his lecture (incidentally, he never once referred to notes but spoke extemporaneously for seven hours), he talked about "giving and caring." His premise was that most of America's great institutions came from the church and that it's not possible to maintain a civil society without the proper use of money. He asked, "How do Americans see money?" Then he answered his own question: "Americans see almost everything about money as nuts and bolts—how to make it, invest it, and spend it. Rarely are we taught how to give it. Thus, the nuts-and-bolts mentality gives rise to philanthropy but only in terms of 'we give to get.'"

Os pointed out that Christians need to ask more important questions: What is the *meaning* of money? Why give? Why care?

At that point he made a comment that, to me, was the

most important one of the whole day: "We give because we have been given to."

I loved that comment, and it makes perfect sense. It's the Good Samaritan parable changing the world. We give because we've been given to, not because it all belongs to God in the first place. Financial acts of community may enhance (or change) our quality of life, but only acts of charity honor God. In other words, it's the heart that has to change in order for someone to see money as honoring to God.

GENEROSITY BEGETS GENEROSITY

The principle underlying this kind of giving is found in Luke 6:38: "Give, and it will be given to you: good measure, pressed down, shaken together, and running over will be put into your bosom. For with the same measure that you use, it will be measured back to you" (NKJV). Eugene Peterson puts it even better in *The Message*: "Give away your life; you'll find life given back, but not merely given back—given back with bonus and blessing. Giving, not getting, is the way. Generosity begets generosity."

Generosity begets generosity. We give because we've been given to.

As a young girl I was taught to tithe, something that

was practiced by my parents and supported by Scripture. Tithing is a timeless principle, meant for every age. It was incorporated into Mosaic Law as well as the New Testament church. Nevertheless, no one had pointed out to me the idea of giving because we've been given to until I heard Os Guinness speak. Giving money out of that foundational motive frees the giver to operate completely out of grace. If those compelled by the law gave one-tenth of their earnings, how much more are we compelled to give out of grace? Romans 6:15 asks, "What then? Shall we sin because we are not under law but under grace? Certainly not!" (NKJV).

Let me encourage you to read 2 Corinthians 9:6–15. The passage lays out very clearly this whole idea of generosity, culminating in verses 10–11: "This most generous God who gives seed to the farmer that becomes bread for your meals is more than extravagant with you. He gives you something you can then give away, which grows into full-formed lives, robust in God, wealthy in every way, so that you can be generous in every way, producing with us great praise to God" (MSG). Can you see how this principle sets a person free?

When I started giving in this manner, I felt liberated from societal rules about giving. I read Stephen Olford's words, which say that God *demands* our tithes. He *deserves* our offerings. When we do this, he *defends* our savings and *defrays* our expenses.[1]

That principle worked! I began thinking about all the things made by God that give something to me: the sun, moon, stars, trees, sea, birds, air, earth—not to mention friends, family, work, music, art, and on and on—and I found I wanted to give on the same basis. I chose programs that had needs I could fill. I wanted to give to others who were engaged in projects based on private financial support. I wanted to help friends to travel abroad, remodel their homes, go to school, and see a doctor.

Last year I even hired a probate attorney to draw up a new will to incorporate a fund into which money would go at my death to be distributed to different charities by the executrix of the will. I wanted to set in motion something that would benefit others, even after I go to be with the Lord. As I've often said, "I can't do everything, but I can do something." And I can tell you from experience, it is inexplicable but true—it *is* better to give than to receive. And it's a lot more fun!

WHY DO WE HOLD BACK?

In May 2006 I spent about an hour and a half in a small meeting with the Irish rock star Bono. As a member of the Data One campaign (a new charitable effort by Americans to rally other Americans one by one to fight the emergency of global AIDS and extreme poverty), I was invited to participate with eight other people to hear Bono's hopes and plans for this movement. I love Bono! He's a believer in Jesus Christ and a philanthropic giant. He encouraged all of us as Americans to help raise the awareness of worldwide concerns and to give to others because we've been given to.

In part, he said, "It is the job of the church to present a plumb line on what is happening in your country. Religiosity in the USA is hypocritical. Only 6 percent of Americans respond to the AIDS crisis, and you're the richest country in the world."

Bono is right. Why do those statistics have to be? We have the ways and means to come to the aid of other countries because of the blessings that have been ours. And, as believers, we have the privilege to give to those less fortunate than we. Why do we hesitate or hold back?

A. W. Tozer addressed this concept about giving freely when he wrote the following:

Earthly possessions can be turned into heavenly treasures. It's like this: A twenty-dollar bill, useless in itself, can be transmuted into milk and eggs and fruit to feed hungry children. Physical and mental powers, valuable in themselves, can be transmuted into still higher values, such as a home and an education for a growing family. Human speech, a very gift of God to mankind, can become consolation for the bereaved or hope for the disconsolate, and it can rise higher and break into prayer and praise of the Most High God.

As base a thing as money often is, it yet can be transmuted into everlasting treasure. It can be converted into food for the hungry and clothing for the poor; it can keep a missionary actively winning lost men to the light of the gospel and thus transmute itself into heavenly values.

Any temporal possession can be turned into everlasting wealth. Whatever is given to Christ is immediately touched with immortality.[2]

LIVING OUT THE GOLDEN RULE

There's nothing like surprising people with a financial gift they least expect. Invite them to do something they couldn't do for themselves, and you pay for it. Think about what you might want or need, and give that very thing to them. It's the Golden Rule multiplied again and again. I can tell you from experience that it will make you happier than you can imagine and get you out of the rut of percentage giving. Make it sacrificial, and don't look back to count the cost. Do it unto the Lord, and see what He does to multiply it, both to the recipient and to you, the giver. You can't ever second-guess His provision. He's full of surprises.

And as Tozer said, this truth doesn't apply only to money. It applies to time, energy, investment, opportunity, position, and care. Giving back to God doesn't make Him any richer, but it makes me, the recipient, more than a dead-end receptacle. It frees me to be all I can be because I'm truly alive by means of a life that flows back to God. Let me give you an example of how this works:

In April 2001 I went to India with five other women from the Women of Faith team through our affiliation with World Vision. Child sponsorship started there in 1960, establishing twenty-three homes for boys and girls who had no place to live. The number of sponsored children back then was 992. By the end of the 1970s, World Vision donors had increased that number to 20,290 children, providing for each child an education, immunization, nutritional food, and the basic necessities of life. During the 1980s, World Vision added to that outreach clean drinking water, skills training, and development projects; the sponsorship rose to 73,105 children. The organization even offered training in beekeeping and poultry- and pig-raising. Everything was right on the level where people lived.

During the next decade, World Vision responded to crises—floods, droughts, and earthquakes—as well as initiated area-development programs to help rural villages and urban areas. The organization addressed issues such as child labor, street children, HIV/AIDS, and female infanticide. And now in 2006, donors enable the group to sponsor more than 85,000 Indian children.

Just before our departure for India, two women from our staff (Stacey Sprague and Libby Baird) were there on another mission trip and were caught in the epicenter of a 7.9 earthquake in Bhuj. On January 26 their hotel fell in! Shock waves were felt all over the country from Bhuj to Calcutta to Chennai to Bombay. And World Vision immediately went to work, digging in the rubble, finding missing persons, providing food and water, and burying the dead. Representatives of the organization assisted more than seventy-five thousand people in forty-two villages with a ninety-day food supply and included tents, blankets, soap, cooking pots, plates, cups, and bowls.

Stacey and Libby were not injured in the earthquake, and when they returned, they were on national television, reporting about the outstanding work of World Vision and its tireless efforts to make a difference.

While we were there in April of that same year, we visited an HIV/AIDS clinic operated by World Vision. The project was initiated to commemorate the life and work of Mother Teresa. She had given so much to the people there, World Vision wanted to give back to others in her honor. (There's our principle on giving again.) This clinic, which opened in 1999, offers care and support to poor and marginalized women and children who have HIV or AIDS and are facing destitution. We met the director of this facility, a beautiful young Indian psychiatrist named Dr. Punitha. She introduced us to all the women and their children. We were very moved by what we saw and the stories we heard. They danced for us and gave their testimonies.

Later that night in our hotel, we heard the stories of three other darling young women who had been rescued from poverty and deprivation by means of sponsorship through World Vision. We met them for dinner and spent the evening together. All in their twenties, Pamela Vijay, Mitcy Fernando, and Michelle D'Sylva were amazing. Since childhood they had been friends who were sponsored by World Vision. Can you imagine how grateful they were for the people who came their way years before, willing to give as they did? Each girl was working on a master's degree in college: Pamela in sociology, Mitcy in physics, and Michelle in psychiatry. They had been pals in grade school, and now they are even closer. They have their futures to look forward to . . . all because of an organization that saved their lives.

That night Thelma Wells asked what they were most grateful for as a result of having a World Vision sponsor.

Pamela said, "Before WV came along we were in total darkness. We had no hope, no light. Nobody seemed to care." Pointing to a candle on the table, she said, "We were like that candle before it was lit . . . just there, idle, unable to do anything for ourselves. But when WV came along and lit the candle, we came to life. It was like we were set free. Somebody gave us a light in the darkness, and it changed our lives forever. It was wonderful!"

Each of these girls expressed such gratitude. They knew they would not be where they were that day had it not been for someone who set them free from the darkness of their lives. I asked Mitcy why she majored in physics. "It's such a hard discipline of study," I said.

"Oh no," she replied. "Everything begins with a particle, and I like learning where it goes from there."

What a superb answer, I thought, *so interested in the details of life.*

Michelle, the psychiatry major, was also a singer. We suggested the little band in the restaurant play "Purify My Heart" so she could sing it, but they'd never heard of it. When they stopped to take a break, however, we persuaded Michelle to get up and sing. Michelle went to the microphone and sang the song without accompaniment. It was unforgettable and so beautiful.

The country of India suffers from a tremendous lack of resources. There is barely enough of anything, and poverty is evident everywhere. But here were these lovely young women, who had received with grateful hearts what they had been given, and they now have so much to give back. We sat in that room spellbound by their stories and their spirits—receiving the great abundance of their hearts. Only God!

World Vision gives this description of its work in India:

> We have seen the face of hunger and shared a
> meal.
> We have felt the anguish of homelessness and
> given a roof.
> We have heard the cry of children and promised a
> future.
> We have seen the darkness of ignorance and
> lighted a lamp.
> We have touched the wounds of the sick and got
> them well.
> We have held the hands of the dying and instilled
> strength.
> We have heard the voice of despair and provided
> world vision.[3]

I witnessed the benefits of all of these accomplishments in action, and I can tell you for a fact that World Vision is setting captives free from every one of these problems. The organization does it well because the participants live out of the goodness of giving and caring. People who have been bound are set free. Not only that, but the givers receive in even greater measure.

Unbelievable, but it's what the Bible says will happen . . . and it does.

I challenge you to find a worthy cause in which you can become involved. We all ride the tide of those who have gone before—those who have left a legacy of giving and caring about others. Perhaps it's something in your own neighborhood, or it could be on the other side of the world. Whatever and wherever it is, join up and start giving. Very few people can change the face of a nation, but everybody can change the face of a neighborhood . . . one person at a time. And in the process, we too are changed.

Choosing Between Yes and No

*Making choices that lead
out of bondage and into liberty*

Some years ago, my friend Kathy was having second thoughts about whether or not she should get married. She was young, attractive, and well educated. She'd graduated from college with honors, earning a degree in German. Her schooling had equipped her to hold a job with one of the major airlines, traveling all over the world. After she'd been employed about a year and a half, a ministerial student she was dating asked her to marry him. It seemed to me to be a perfect match because I knew Kathy was a strong Christian with high principles who had a lot to offer a husband. Her quandary occurred over whether she wanted to give up the single life.

One day, in one of our many conversations about this time of uncertainty and confusion, I said to her, "Kathy, what is the primary reason for your hesitation in marrying Warren? He's a great guy. I know you love him and feel he's the person with whom you could share the rest of your life. What's the deal? What's keeping you from saying yes?"

Please understand I wasn't trying to pry or force anything that Kathy didn't want to talk about. We were very good friends, and this type of probing characterized our relationship. Her answer was interesting, and I've thought about it many years hence.

"Well, Luci," she said, "if I say yes to Warren, it's a very big yes, affecting my life from now on. But if I say no, it's equally big, and I realize that whatever I say, I've given up one thing to have the other. By saying a conscious yes, I've automatically said no to something else. It's such an important decision, I want to weigh the consequences. What will yes bring with it . . . and what will saying no bring?"

Her response to my question not only demonstrated a lot about Kathy's character but also served as a valid commentary on decision making that is rarely reduced to words. Kathy had to make up her mind about a very serious matter, and she wanted to do it with tremendous care because the consequences would accompany her the remainder of her life. Incidentally, Kathy ultimately said yes to Warren, and they've been happily married for many years and have a wonderful family.

When we enter the adult world, leaving behind our childhood with its innocence and naïveté, we soon find that the art of living life—any lifestyle of our choosing—is a full-time occupation and responsibility. There are values to be established, obligations to be met, decisions to be made, and crosses to be borne. We begin to see for ourselves that few situations are ideal. There are numerous adjustments we have to make daily in order to cope with what is real, and there is no escaping reality with its need for concessions, compromises, and risks.

ADJUSTING OPPOSING ISSUES

Outside the restriction of our parents' instruction, we must choose for ourselves what paths we want to follow with the understanding that each time we say yes to one thing, we automatically say no to something else, often without conscious thought. We learn that we simply cannot have everything we want in life and we cannot be free of confusion about decision making until we learn to give up one thing to have another. We must constantly learn how to adjust opposing demands and issues. To live in the real world, we will always need to surrender some position of thought or action in order to find the freedom to fully embrace the other. In short, we can't have our cake and eat it too.

In his book *The Myth of Certainty,* Daniel Taylor writes,

Being human is a risky business. This is a basic, undisputed truth. . . . At every point we are confronted with the breach between the longings of our heart and the limits of our situation. No significant area of our life is free from risk. It is a key ingredient in every accomplishment and every relationship. Whenever a decision is required, there is risk. Wherever we must act, there is risk. Wherever people intertwine their lives, there is risk.[1]

I read Dr. Taylor's book the year it was first published, and during that summer (1986), I started thinking about a possibility that would alter the course of my life forever. I needed to answer the question, Should I retire from Mobil Oil Corporation? I had worked for the company twenty-nine years. But I was also engaged in a speaking ministry and writing my third book. I was on a collision course. One of my activities was eventually going to crash into the others with a mighty blast, but I didn't want to give up any of them. And which should I stop doing? Each one was satisfying and challenging. I felt trapped, so I spent lots of time trying to decide which should get a yes and which should get a no. As Daniel

Taylor said, I kept thinking about the breach between the longings of my heart and the limits of my situation. *What should I do?*

I worked on a plan to get my spirit free of the bondage I was feeling. I made notes in my journal. I talked with those I trusted and asked their counsel. I tried to imagine every possible result should I say, "Yes, I'm going to retire while I'm ahead. This is a good age," as opposed to, "No, I cannot retire. I'm too young. How will I make a living?"

Probably the best thing I did was to make lists. Oh, my! I made dozens of lists—about money, goals, fears, dreams, lifestyle, debts, friends, travel, and spiritual quandaries—and I laid them all before God, seeking His advice and direction. I wrote quotations and scriptures that became sources of encouragement, sticking them strategically around my house and office. Here are a few of them:

The world is round and the place which may seem like the end may also be the beginning. Ivy Baker Priest, (1905–75)

He holds our lives in his hands. And he holds our feet to the path. (Psalm 66:9 TLB)

Time is the coin of our lives. We must take care how we spend it. Carl Sandburg (1878–1967)

Search the Book of the Lord and see all that he will do.
(Isaiah 34:16 TLB)

*Delight yourself in the LORD; and He will give you the
desires of your heart.*" (Psalm 37:4 NASB)

*Don't be anxious about tomorrow. God will take care
of your tomorrow too.* (Matthew 6:34 TLB)

*A decision is the action an executive must take when
he has information so incomplete that the answer
does not suggest itself.* Arthur William Radford
(1896–1973)

I especially loved the final quotation because that was
exactly where I found myself. The information about my
future was so incomplete that the answer was unclear at
best. I was completely dependent upon God and what He
wanted to do with my life, which at times seemed very
remote and beyond my comprehension. Of course, this
has been true since I was born, but its relevancy had
never hit me in the face as it did during those months of
trying to decide between yes and no. (Incidentally, I saved
all those quotations and scriptures in my 1987 journal,
and I reread them today, twenty years later. They're just
as timely.)

CAN GOD TAKE CARE OF ME?

As the days and weeks of 1986 turned into 1987, I slowly began to have a clear picture of what I should do. I didn't want to stop working for Mobil until I had secured a way of making a living other than speaking and writing (both being somewhat sporadic), but I determined that if God led me in that direction, I'd try my best to have the faith to do it. It was hard to contradict the teaching of my dad (always have the next thing in mind before moving ahead), but I wanted to completely let go of everything that would hinder my full trust in the Lord. And it was to that end that I prayed.

Oh, there was something else: I had always been employed where I got a paycheck from an office. Granted, the money I received for speaking came independently, but I didn't consider that "my real job." Speaking was a sort of sideline to where I really worked. I made a living at Mobil, but I made a life when I was speaking and writing. In other words, my Mobil checks paid for the rent, the utility bills, the health insurance, the credit card bills, the groceries, and so forth. The checks from speaking were extra—not something I could control or depend on.

I really had to talk to the Lord about this because it became a barrier when I wanted to let go of everything yet saw the lack of guaranteed income as the reason to stay with Mobil. Even though I sensed God leading me away from the corporate world, I kept asking myself, *Can God take care of me?* Of course, I had seen Him do it again and again while I had that eight-to-five job, but practically speaking, how was He going to do it if I gave up the job? I wanted to know His plan in advance so I could look at it, think it over, edit it, and be sure it fit me. *Hmmm . . . big roadblock!*

About that time, I found the most phenomenal quotation. It changed everything. I have no idea where it originated or the exact day I read it, but it made me decide to take the big plunge and retire in 1987. In a nutshell, it said something along these lines:

If you laugh, you might look like a fool, and if you cry, you'll be too sentimental. If you help another person . . . are you sure you want to get involved? Anytime you show your true feelings, people will see inside of you. If you let other people know your ideas or tell them your dreams, you run the risk of losing both. Even when you love somebody, he or she might not love you back. Living, hoping, trying . . . all of that involves risk.

But you've got to take risks because it's even worse to risk nothing. If you don't risk, you'll do nothing, have nothing, and be nothing. You might avoid getting hurt or being embarrassed, but how will you ever grow or change or love or—most of all—how will you *live*? You'll be chained by trying to be certain about everything, and nobody can be certain. Those chains will take away your freedom. Is that what you want?

The piece ended with, "Only the person who risks is free."

When I read that, I felt a euphoric high, like I was walking on air. I could have tried to figure out God's plan all day, but in the end I simply had to trust. When I read "only the person who risks is free," I knew I wanted that freedom, and to get it, I had to take the risk. That did it for me! God had promised to lead me, and I really started feeling His leading in spite of traces of insecurity and fear. It was obvious I had to say no to one thing to have another, but saying yes to retirement started a ball rolling that has not stopped to this day . . . twenty years later. No matter what, I was on the path to freedom, and I could *feel* it in my spirit.

On Sunday night, May 17, 1987, my sister-in-law Cynthia Swindoll called and asked if I would consider going to work for Insight for Living (IFL), my brother's international Christian ministry. She had no idea I was thinking of taking early retirement. Nevertheless, out of the blue she placed that call and asked if I would be interested in being vice president of public relations for IFL. Note: this did *not* happen prior to my decision to retire; it happened after I had decided to cut the "chains of my certitudes" and take the risk to trust God for whatever happened. That's huge to me because it's so much easier to take a plunge when we know where we're going to land instead of jumping into thin air and trusting God to catch us.

I could hardly believe her call. It was such a confirmation of Isaiah 54:2: "Enlarge the place of your tent . . . do not hold back; lengthen your cords." I knew my dedication had to be expanded so that I would leave everything to follow Him. Not an easy place to be for one who is accustomed to independence of my own making and prefers control.

I retired from Mobil in September 1987 and began that same month with Insight for Living. For five years I reported to that office and did a bit of freelance speaking. That period served as an excellent transition from the corporate world into a full-time world of speaking and writing. Now I never report to an office, and the Lord has proven Himself completely faithful in taking care of me financially. Amazingly, He has met me at every turn and in every way . . . repeatedly keeping His word about taking care of "all my tomorrows." In fact, just recently He reiterated His promise that I will always be free when I find my solace in Him. Here's what happened:

I was in Israel with a group of six hundred listeners of Insight for Living, including Chuck and Cynthia, and several members of the Women of Faith speaking team. It was a wonderful trip. While we were in a boat on the Sea of Galilee, Chuck was speaking one morning and challenged us to give our deepest burden to the Lord. He had instructed each of us to bring a rock on board, and he suggested that each one's rock was to be a symbol of a personal burden. He gave us several moments of silence to consider the things that might be bothering us, and when we felt like it, he urged us to throw the burden-holding rock overboard and listen to it hit the water, then recognize that it would sink to the bottom of the sea.

"It can be anything," he said, "some habit you need to break, a grudge you need to get beyond, a dream you need to let go of, a fear you need to conquer." He listed numerous possibilities. And once again, I thought of my future. As I get older, it's easy to fret about health, age, flagging energies, and lack of physical strength in light of all the demands on my life as one who travels all the time—constant packing and unpacking, time changes, and all the inconveniences that go along with that. There are many questions that accompany the aging process, and I don't know the answer to any of them.

So I sat on that boat thinking, *Should I give God the burden of travel? Should I give Him my health concerns? Should I take on more responsibility in other areas of my life? Should I be more involved in my church or neighborhood?* And it occurred to me that I should simply give Him my future, whatever that might look like—once again, turn it all over to Him if I want to be free. *Take the plunge, Luci. Let go of whatever is on your horizon as that rock plunges into the Sea of Galilee.*

And that's exactly what I did.

Since that morning I've had that same, wonderful, euphoric high I experienced twenty years ago when I said no to Mobil and yes to early retirement. It's made me free of concern for my future. I'm open to any transition that comes my way because I know whatever it is, He is in charge. What a load off!

Daniel Taylor says, "Without this freedom, commitment would be inconceivable, since the concept only has meaning when there is the possibility of doing otherwise."[2] We have to choose with our wills that we want God to be in control of our lives, and when we do that, He takes the weight off our shoulders and puts it on His own. God assured us:

> I have created you and cared for you since you were born. I will be your God through all your lifetime, yes, even when your hair is white with age. (Isaiah 46:3–4 TLB)

That works for me! I'm looking at my life from the "other side of the hill." I now have the white hair Isaiah speaks of, and I can tell you from experience that the Lord is certainly with me, caring for me just as He did when I was a child. I can feel it every day in a thousand ways. He gives me joy and purpose and a true sense of freedom. It's a great way to live.

9

Waiting and Not Waiting

*Learning the value of
being able to do both*

In early April 2006, I had a car accident. I'd left home about 5:30 p.m. to run to the post office—a simple errand I do often. It was a bright, sunshiny afternoon ... great weather ... and I was going to dash down there and come right back. I'd told my friends I'd bring all of us a Starbucks, and we'd sit on Marilyn's patio and visit until sundown. As usual, my plan was in place.

When I got to the corner of Lebanon Road and Parkwood, I needed to make a left turn to go north. Approaching the turn signal that showed a green arrow for my direction, I confidently moved forward.

Just as I nosed into the intersection, however, the arrow went off, but because my light was still green and the oncoming cars didn't move, I assumed I was good to go. Not so.

About three-quarters into that intersection, I was struck by a car coming toward me at full speed out of the far lane. The woman was distracted, didn't stop at her light, was blinded by the setting sun, was confused by the five o'clock traffic, was careless in her driving, or *something*. But she crashed into me on the front-right fender, and both our cars sustained a great deal of damage. Especially mine. Her vehicle's front grille fell in the street and the bumper was dragging, but my car was in much worse shape. The entire suspension system had been moved to the left, and almost everything from the firewall forward had to be replaced: hood, bumper, grille, radiator, fender, headlights, wheel, tire, and numerous parts in the engine.

"It's a mess," the tow-truck driver said later. "And it's a wonder you're not hurt."

Once the other driver and I realized we were able to get out of our cars and step to the side of the road, we exchanged insurance information as both of us kept saying the same thing: "I had a green light."

We looked around, assessed the damage to the degree we could, and called the police, who arrived within about thirty minutes. "We would have been here earlier," one of the officers said, "but we were working on a robbery in the mall." A busy day for those guys!

It's been months now since that little episode, but immediately thereafter I experienced severe bruising and a hematoma in my right breast, a knot on my right knee and thigh, a detached retina in my right eye, the loosening of two fillings in my teeth, and a slight fear of driving a car. It took me awhile to get back to normal but less time than it took my car, which was under repair at the dealership for fifty days. (But who's counting?)

Every day my car was in the shop I thought about the accident as I slowly began to heal from those various injuries. A couple of times I even dreamed about it and awakened in a shudder at the moment of impact. In my mind's eye I saw that car coming toward me out of my peripheral vision but couldn't do anything except sit there and receive the blow. It all happened in five or six seconds. Neither of us got a ticket, and the police report (which represented both of us accurately) didn't say either of us did anything wrong. For months I repeatedly asked myself, *Was that wreck my fault?* I don't know and, of course, never will.

I do know one thing, though. Had I waited, it would not have happened. And if I had it to do over, I would wait. The little phrase "I had a green light" holds the key to my instinct to pull into the intersection.

IF ONLY WE HAD WAITED . . .

How many times in life do we move ahead, then wish we hadn't? It's not that we're purposely throwing caution to the wind or being indifferent to what's best; it's that we assume we have the right-of-way. For whatever reason we have our plan in place. We want to go, and nothing can stop us. Because of that plan, we have the misconception we can do anything we want to. We feel free. In hindsight, I realize going into that intersection was the wrong course of action, but it's too late. The deed is done, and the consequences are mine to live with. I had never been involved in a car accident of this magnitude, and yet, could it have been avoided?

Did it happen to teach me a lesson about my driving? Maybe. I certainly think twice now when I'm behind the wheel, and it's made me more cautious in almost every area of my life. It's made me stop and think, whether consciously or unconsciously. For the time being anyway, I don't automatically go on green. I'm more cautious because I want to be sure.

Are you familiar with the book *Blink: The Power of Thinking without Thinking*, published in 2005? Malcolm Gladwell, the author, has given his readers an interesting treatise on the value of decision making in the blink of an eye. He calls it "thin-slicing," where one is able to rapidly filter the most pertinent factors that matter from an overwhelming number of variables in order to reach a split-second conclusion. Gladwell believes this ability to make quick judgments can be enjoyed by everybody, not just those who have the "gift." He says,

> Just as we teach ourselves to think logically and deliberately, we can also teach ourselves to make better snap judgments.... The power of knowing, in that first two seconds, is not a gift given magically to a fortunate few. It is an ability that we can all cultivate for ourselves.[1]

I've learned to trust this experience as the leading of the Spirit. When we walk with God, according to His way, we can trust Him to show us what to do in decision making. Even snap judgments become more accurate when we live in an attitude of trusting God. In other words, the more truth we know and apply in our lives about how God leads and how His Spirit works, the more we're able to trust the precision of quick decisions. God uses His Spirit to transform our lives so that our thoughts are constantly being conformed to His way of thinking.

Snap decisions can actually save our lives.

As you read in the previous chapter, I was employed by Mobil Oil Corporation for thirty years, and the last eleven of those years, I worked in Torrance, California, at West Coast Pipelines. Seven of those years I was an agent in the Rights-of-Way and Claims Department, and during the last four, I was the department manager, from which I took early retirement in 1987.

While I was an agent, my responsibility was to negotiate with various property owners for terms and conditions regarding pipeline easements. Often this involved appearing before a city council meeting at night. In the late 1970s during the Iranian hostage crisis, when there were long lines of cars waiting to get gas at service stations across the country and everybody pretty much hated the petroleum industry because of these shortages, it fell my lot to go to one of these meetings in the city of Norwalk. I needed to negotiate for three miles of pipeline that had been operating perfectly for many years, but because the franchise was about to expire, I wanted to try to secure it for more years to come.

My desire was to work out a deal with the city for a renewal "in perpetuity," but short of that, for at least twenty-five years. (Secretly, I thought if we could just keep that pipeline active long enough for me to retire soon, I'd at least be off the scene and somebody else could inherit that headache.)

So off I went on a cold, rainy night in November to do Mobil business in Norwalk, feeling fairly defeated before I left home, considering the nature of my petition and knowing the world already hated oil companies and anybody who worked for them. I walked in the back of the meeting room, which was filled with people. I presented my name and cause to the city clerk (that I would be asking for twenty-five more years of pipeline in their city streets), then found a seat near the back and waited my turn.

When I sat down, I noticed a man across the aisle looking straight at me. The whole time I was sitting there, he stared and frowned and kept rolling up a newspaper or magazine in front of him, never taking his eyes off me. Needless to say, his behavior unnerved me, but I tried to ignore it as I waited—and prayed: "Father, I don't know who this guy is across the aisle, but please protect me. Why is he staring at me?"

About eight thirty the council called for the business from Mobil Oil Corporation and asked the representative to stand, introduce herself, and be prepared to answer questions (if there were any). As I stood, faced the panel of council members, and gave my name, I noticed again out of the corner of my eye the newspaper-roller to my right, but I tried to maintain my composure and concentrate on the matter before the council. Strangely enough, when my petition was read aloud, no one asked a single question, and the request for another twenty-five years passed with no objection. Hallelujah! I was thrilled.

I thanked the mayor and gathered up my things to leave. As I turned to walk out of the row, I realized the stranger across the aisle was no longer there, and that *really* bothered me. I asked myself, *Now, where is that dude? Where did he go? Is he outside this door waiting for me? Is he going to find me? Does he have a gun or knife inside that newspaper? Is he going to kill me?*

When I got outside, there was a fine mist in the air, and it was colder than when I arrived. But I breathed a sigh of relief . . . nobody was waiting for me. I turned up my collar and kept walking toward my car. When I left the lighted area of the city hall, I had to walk down a dark path about two hundred yards long covered with overhanging trees. Out from behind a tree popped the man with the rolled-up paper. It was now just him and me. He stood right in front of me, invading my space and blocking me from going farther. Only his hands and the rolled newspaper were between us. Very quietly and intently, he said, "You the representative from the oil company?"

I swallowed hard. "Yes, I am," I answered. I had no idea what was going to happen next, but I feared the worst.

He started in on a string of filthy expletives, calling me every name in the book, even some I'd never heard of, and ending with a diatribe that was one long, badgering sentence interspersed with colorful, four-letter words as he got closer and closer to my face: "You're the reason we can't get oil or gas, aren't you? I have a fleet of trucks that I can't get gas for and it's you and your company who are putting me out of business and there's going to be an uprising in this country and I'm going to lead it and the first person I'm going to kill is you and there's nothing you can do about it. So what do you think of that?"

Let me step out of that picture here for a minute to say this: at that point I obviously needed a "blink" comeback. I had to say something, but I had no idea what. Any suggestions from the reader?

Amazingly, I was very calm. Who knows why? The whole time he was talking, I was saying (in my head) one long sentence of my own, including things like, *I will keep you in perfect peace when your mind is stayed on Me*, and *Peace I give to you*, and *Trust in the Lord with all your heart* . . . and even, *Though He slay me, yet will I trust in Him* . . . anything I could think of from the Bible.

So, when the guy took a breath, guess what I said that just popped out of my mouth? It came from somewhere inside me, but I have no idea where. I "blinked" and heard myself say, "Excuse me, sir, but do you have a business card?"

Where did that line come from? It must have been from God because immediately, the paper-roller was so completely disarmed, he looked at me a few seconds then lowered his hands, stepped backward, reached in his pocket, took out his billfold, and opened it. (Incidentally, it was bulging with money.) He removed a beat-up, old, dirty business card and handed it to me.

The card said something like, "Jim Swift, president . . . Swift Trucking Company." Below that, the vice president's name had been marked out with a pen.

He probably killed that guy and is just too cheap to buy new cards.

I thanked him for his card and asked if I could take it with me to work the next day. He stepped back farther and said, "Well . . . sure." I told him I was so sorry about his inconvenience regarding the gas he couldn't buy, but that the petroleum industry had nothing to do with that. "Decisions regarding distribution of oil and gas products are made by OPEC, but I will promise you one thing, Mr. Swift: I'll personally call the president of Mobil Oil tomorrow, and I'll let you know what I find out. You have my word."

There were a couple more rude comments from him, to which I said nothing, then I finally asked, "May I go, please? It's raining, and I need to get home. If you'll excuse me, I'll call you tomorrow. I have your card. Thank you. Good night."

As I was walking away and my back was to him, he yelled, "What's your name again?"

"Swindoll—Luci Swindoll." I kept walking.

Then he yelled, "Swindle! That's a good name for you," to which I responded, "Yes, sir! I guess it's all in how it's pronounced," and went to my car as he turned and left.

Once I sat down in the car and slammed the door, I

fell apart. I cried and cried. I felt my heart beating out of my chest and thanked God I was still alive. I haven't a clue what that man was rolling up inside the paper and what he'd planned to do to me had I not had that split-second response about the business card. But I did. It was God's Spirit blended with my sixth sense. I drove directly to Marilyn and Ken's house and told them the whole thing. We all praised God together that I was alive, in my right mind, and able to tell the story. They were very comforting, and I was very relieved.

Here's what is strange about that whole story: I had no idea who in the world the president of Mobil Oil Corporation was, but I found out quickly the next day. I told my buddies what happened, and they dubbed me "Cool Hand Luci." But they all agreed, "You can't call the president of Mobil . . . he probably lives on Mars. Call the PR manager in Los Angeles. He'll know what to do." I talked with our LA rep for a long time about the whole problem, and he kindly offered to call Mr. Swift for me.

"No, I'll do it . . . but thank you. I promised I'd call him myself, and I need to keep my word." I needed to tell Mr. Swift I couldn't talk with the president of Mobil, but I had information from our PR manager that might be helpful.

Mr. Swift's secretary answered and said he wasn't in. I told her who I was and explained that he and I had talked the night before. I gave her the reason for my call and asked her to have him call me back. To this day, he has not phoned. That was about thirty years ago, so it's doubtful he'll call me now.

HOW DO WE REACH CERTAINTY?

While God gave me the quick response that saved me from that ominous situation, I can also remember many times when I've had to learn to wait, even though I wanted to keep moving ahead—building a home, spending money for travel, investing in stock—all major decisions about which I was uncertain. In each case I thought, pondered, prayed, and trusted and experienced countless hours of uncertainty, but finally, certainty came. How did that happen?

God moves at His own pace. Sometimes He appears in a split second; other times He takes forever. I've often said, "God may be slow, but He's never a moment late." The car wreck is an example of a careless, distracted running ahead. The Mobil account is an example of how He leads when we have no idea what to say or do. Either way, He's with us. We have the freedom to choose for ourselves, but here's what I want to do . . . if I can just remember it:

Trust GOD from the bottom of your heart;
don't try to figure out everything on your own.

Listen for GOD's voice in everything you do,
everywhere you go;
he's the one who will keep you on track.
(Proverbs 3:4–5 MSG)

10

Receiving More When You Already Have Enough

Escaping the insatiable cravings of your heart

Two years after I graduated from college, my parents gave me my first "serious" Bible. Before that time I had had a small white one that I'd won in Vacation Bible School for memorizing the books of the Bible in proper order. I also had various New Testaments from different friends and a Bible I'd bought when I got my first job, but *this* Bible was the real McCoy. It was the Scofield Reference Edition Bible, printed in 1945 and given to me in 1957, fifty years ago. Brown leather with my name engraved in gold on the front . . . Lucille Swindoll.

My mother had written the sweetest inscription in front that read, in part:

June 1957
Honey,

May you remember all the precious things that this Book contains as you study it day by day. Go forth to bear the fruit of a holy life to the glory of God so that your life may praise Him. Go forward in the name and by the strength of Him in whom all things are possible and easy and safe.

Mighty opportunities of good lie along the narrow, thorn-set path of obedience to the Word and will of God. "The battle is the Lord's," so let Him have His way in your life . . . The Christian life is begun, grows, continues and conquers only by faith!

Keep trusting Him, the Lord Jesus Christ . . . We love you,

Mother and Daddy

I've loved that Bible and studied it for many years. Even as I write this now, I'm looking at it—frayed, tattered, marked up, yellowed with age, and more precious to me than the day my folks gave it to me. Even though I have a shelf full of Bibles now, last Sunday I took this old one to church as I often do because I love the feel of it in my hands and because I understand my markings and can find them blindfolded. That Bible is so familiar to me; it's an extension of my arm and hand. I don't want to have it recovered and spiffed up. I can't bear to lose the patina it's acquired from years of love and use.

Nineteen fifty-seven was the year I started seriously going four nights a week to a Bible class where I began to learn many new truths. My teacher, a strong proponent of God's grace, taught that Christ was born under the law, lived under the law, died under the law, and was the end of the law . . . and by virtue of those facts, everybody born after Christ's resurrection was no longer living under the law but in the dispensation of the church age. That means all of us have the opportunity to enjoy a life of freedom through grace, not performance through legalism: "Christ has set us free to live a free life" (Galatians 5:1 MSG).

Let me just stop here for a quick aside and say, "Hallelujah!" That's the best news in the world. (If Marilyn can stop for giggle breaks, surely you'll allow me to pause for occasional "Hallelujahs!")

DISCOVERING THE TREASURE TROVE

In that little Bible class I learned from Hebrews 6 that I could grow in knowledge beyond the basics of salvation.

Christ died for my sins, but that's just the beginning of my treasure trove. Because of the indwelling Holy Spirit, I learned I have the spiritual capacity to understand doctrines, precepts, covenants, spiritual gifts . . . all pertaining to living a full life *after* redemption. I also learned for the first time that to have my sins forgiven, all I had to do was confess them to God, and He was faithful to forgive them and cleanse me from all unrighteousness (see 1 John 1:9). I learned from the book of Romans that the moment I believed in the finished work of Christ on the cross, I was justified by faith, and that Christ declared me "righteous" while I was still in my "sinning state."

That declaration was a sovereign act of God, not something that was predicated on my performance or good behavior. Equally important, I was taught that being justified by grace was not the same as "just as if I'd never sinned," but the exact opposite—the very fact of my sin required Christ to go to the cross on my behalf. Salvation became a personal, relevant, unequivocal act of grace on the part of Christ. To me, realizing that truth was huge; it set me upon a path of study I've continued until this day. It changed everything about my life because it set me free to be totally myself.

And guess what? It can do the same for you.

Little by little I began to understand that a world of gifts became mine at the moment of salvation. No one had ever pointed that out to me before I attended that class. I was over the moon. Nobody in churches I had attended since childhood had ever passed along the information I received in my class. No wonder I attended four nights a week for two years! I simply could not get my fill. I took notes, made little books, drew outlines and charts, memorized scripture, wrote in the margin of my Bible and on the flyleaf, copied everything into a journal, and talked night and day about what I was learning. I had dived headfirst into a sea of priceless pearls that were mine for the taking . . . everything was right in front of me . . . on a silver platter. For the first time I was receiving more when I thought I already had enough!

To serve as a ready reminder of all these riches, my parents suggested I list them in the front of my Bible with scriptures beside each to support that truth. Taking Mother and Daddy seriously, I made the list, and there it is still for me to see and read every day. I wrote down thirty-five things that became mine once I entered the kingdom of God. There are more, but I ran out of writing room. And I've discovered many more as the years have gone by.

That list reminds me I'm a spiritual millionaire, rich in benefits: love from God the Father, fellowship with Christ the Son, and the indwelling of the Holy Spirit, all on a daily basis. As it says in the last few verses of Psalm 46 in my old Bible, "Be still, and know that I am God: I will be exalted among the heathen, I will be exalted in the earth. The LORD of hosts is with us; the God of Jacob is our refuge" (KJV).

Eugene Peterson paraphrases the same thought in *The Message*: "Attention, all! See the marvels of GOD! . . . 'Step out of the traffic! Take a long, loving look at me, your High God, above politics, above everything.'"

That's exactly what happened to me. I stepped "out of the traffic" and took a long, loving look at my high God, and what I found was numberless blessings.

FREED BY A WEALTH OF BLESSINGS

"OK, Luci. How does this help me be free?" you ask.

Well . . . here are a few examples.

I have a "new priesthood" under the grace of God, and not under the Old Testament Law (see Hebrews 7:11, 12 MSG). This means I'm free to pray directly to God without going through another human being to reach Him. I'm free from confessing my sins to anyone other than Christ. I don't have to be embarrassed or ashamed because someone else might know about my sins. Only God needs to know. That's liberating.

I have both Jesus Christ and the Holy Spirit dwelling inside me (see Romans 8:9; Galatians 2:20; Colossians 1:27). This means wherever I go I'm never alone. Christ is in God and I'm in Christ, so we are always together.

Jesus is seated at the right hand of the Father, so I'm there too, because I'm in Him. A great deal of what I do and how I think can be appreciated and/or understood because I have Christ's perspective. And the Holy Spirit is in me to guide my thoughts, actions, behavior, and decisions. The onus of responsibility rests on Him, not on me. That's liberating.

I have a personal relationship with God now, not a religious experience where I have to pull myself up by my own bootstraps to merit His love and attention (Ephesians 5:1–10). This doesn't mean I don't need fellowship with believers like friends in my church. It means I don't have to clean up my act before God can receive me. I can worship Him anywhere, and there's no need for the performing of any kind of ritual prior to coming into His presence through prayer. That's liberating.

I have a reason for going through suffering or difficulty because I have an "eternal inheritance" with God (see 1 Peter 1:3–4; Hebrews 9:15 KJV). This means when I am in the throes of pain or hurt, God knows all about it and gives meaning and purpose to it so I can learn life lessons. Everything that happens has a reason, even though we may not know some of those reasons until we get to heaven! He takes me through these things to refine me and to encourage others later when they go through the same things. He enables me to grow up through difficult times and experience His faithfulness. In the hard times He's with me, no matter where I am or how hard they get. And He has a great plan to take me through this life into the next . . . always with Him. That's liberating.

KEEP GOING, KEEP GROWING

The unfortunate thing about many people in the church today is they don't know how rich they are. Not knowing that salvation is just the beginning, they stop there and never know how much more could be theirs. I believe the human heart is insatiable. No matter what we have, deep inside we always want more. Yet God lays a banquet before us for the taking, and many of us don't know about it, or if we do, we don't go to the trouble to pull up to the table.

Scripture encourages us to keep going . . . keep growing up. It instructs us to receive more, even when we think we have enough. Read Hebrews 6:1–3 from *The Message:*

> So come on, let's leave the preschool fingerpainting exercises on Christ and get on with the grand work of art. Grow up in Christ. The basic foundational truths are in place: turning your back on "salvation

by self-help" and turning in trust toward God; baptismal instructions; laying on of hands; resurrection of the dead; eternal judgment. God helping us, we'll stay true to all that. But there's so much more. Let's get on with it.

There's the key—those four little words, *there's so much more*, and it is to that end that this chapter makes reference. We're getting on with the "grand work of art."

I love art. It was my major in college and continues to be the field of study that most fascinates me. In early 2006 I read an excellent book on art. I've read art books for years and enjoyed them all, but this one takes the cake. It's about seven hundred pages long, and I actually hated for it to end. I hung on every word. Its simple title is *The Story of Art* by E. H. Gombrich. But its content is full to the brim with his brilliant writing. Since the early 1950s this book has sold more than six million copies and is still going strong. Listen to what Gombrich says about what he calls "great works of art," and think about God's pouring Himself into your life when you read these lines. You are becoming God's great painting:

One never finishes learning about art. There are always new things to discover. Great works of art seem to look different every time one stands before them. They seem to be inexhaustible and unpredictable. . . . Nobody should think he knows all about it, for nobody does. Nothing, perhaps, is more important than just this: that to enjoy these works we must have a fresh mind, one which is ready to catch every hint and to respond to every hidden harmony.[1]

Having studied art most of my life, I continue to mine the depths of understanding and insight about all I see and read. If I live to be a hundred, I will want to go to art museums, read art books, and have long discussions with my friends about the world of art. It's my passion. How much more this is true of my faith.

LEARNING TO CATCH GOD'S HIDDEN HARMONIES

God is full of surprises and gives us unique ways to learn about this masterpiece He's developing in us by His Spirit as we grow up in Him. And Gombrich is right: the fresher our minds, the quicker we'll catch God's hidden harmonies all around us. We'll be able to see the rich tapestry God is making of our lives. We might even have times when we actually feel His work being done in us. He'll open new doors we can walk through.

Knowing God is enough, right from the first second we understand He can be known and we put our faith in Him. However, He makes it possible for us to receive more in our understanding and knowledge of Him for the rest of our lives. We do this by knowing God's Word . . . the Bible. We cannot begin to perceive what God has in store for us until we start digesting scripture for ourselves. We have to spend time there, learning, absorbing, applying, and enriching our insufficient, meager lives. In Proverbs 9 of *The Message*, Eugene Peterson captures in a word picture Lady Wisdom's inviting all of us to dinner. She says:

Are you confused about life, don't know what's
   going on?
   Come with me, oh come, have dinner with me!
I've prepared a wonderful spread—fresh-baked
   bread,
   roast lamb, carefully selected wines.
Leave your impoverished confusion and *live*!
   Walk up the street to a life with meaning.

No matter how old we are, every Christian can have a life of meaning. We can understand that everything that happens is designed to enrich us so we can learn and grow up. How will we ever have anything to offer anyone else unless we ourselves change for the better?

It is obvious to me that I have a very rich heritage in faith, for which I'm exceedingly grateful. My parents, their parents, and theirs for generations have been Bible students and teachers. In addition I was born in a country and at a time when people honored Christ for the most part and revered the Bible as a standard for living. The Bible itself was easily accessible for me to study. But what about someone who didn't grow up in a similar setting?

Let me tell you about people who couldn't be more opposite from me and whose life experience couldn't be more different. In 2004 the Women of Faith speaker team went to South Africa with World Vision to learn more about its work regarding sponsorship as well as its involvement with women and children who have been affected by the HIV/AIDS crisis. We were able to see first-hand the devastation within families who had lost loved ones to the ravages of this disease. I will never forget the afternoon we went to the home of a grandmother who had recently lost her son, daughter-in-law, and grandson to AIDS. Their fresh graves were in front of the little hut, and we walked by them in order to go inside.

An entire community of women had gathered to mourn with her, wait with her, grieve with her as the gravity of these losses became a reality. We too sat on the dirt floor or on little benches to be a part of the mourning process. Everything about it was extremely touching and deeply moving. None of the women spoke English, and of course, none of us spoke Zulu. Nevertheless, just by looking at each other and making eye contact, we had a sense of fellowship and communication that went beyond the language barrier.

After a while one of the women on our team suggested we sing. We began that old, familiar hymn "It Is Well with My Soul." We were stunned when all these women joined us in singing it—in their own language. We sang every verse in English as they sang their verses in Zulu. Oh, my! Such solace. There was not a dry eye in the house. Some languages are universal.

It was one of the richest moments of my life. Regardless of circumstances that were unbearable, it was well with our souls, and we all knew it. Because we all knew God was in our midst; we were broken, sorrowful, grieving... and He was there. Language barriers were bridged. Culture barriers were bridged. Status barriers were bridged. Nationality barriers were bridged. We were one in the Spirit of God. All that I knew and had studied, as dear as it is to me, was nothing compared to what I knew in that moment as I communed with women who might have had a Bible, but there wasn't one in sight. God had a way to teach them the reality of faith, and it was not the same way He taught me.

Nothing existed in that moment except our collective spiritual unity. We were all free to be ourselves, expressing the fact that God loves us individually. It was unifying, as it should be when we are one in Christ. Everybody was the richer for having been there that day. I kept thinking, *It's what we value that makes us rich and free, not what we own. We're all spiritual millionaires.*

As much as I had in my heart and soul when I went to South Africa (and by anybody's standard it was more than enough), God gave me, in that moment, abundantly more.

11

Knowing Beyond the Shadow of a Doubt

Living freely by trusting God's promises, precepts, and commandments

Are you a worrier? Do you fret when something doesn't go your way? Do you sit around borrowing trouble, dreaming up things you *think* will happen even when you have no foundational ground that they really will? Then you'll love what I observed a few years ago at the Museum of Modern Art in New York.

Trying to get to all six floors in one afternoon because I had only four hours to devote to that great museum, I had to move pretty fast in front of those marvelous paintings I love so much. I hate to go through a museum with that kind of speed, but rather than not go at all, I decided to rush. Suddenly, something stopped me dead in my tracks. It was a framed piece of vellum with this throwaway comment penciled in the center:

Some days you wake up and immediately start to worry. Nothing in particular is wrong, it's just the suspicion that forces are aligning quietly and there will be trouble.

—Jenny Holzer

That amused me because it captures in a nutshell how we often feel. I decided to hang around a few minutes and watch people's reactions as they read the comment. First of all, *everybody* stopped. Second, *everybody* laughed. And third, *everybody* commented. Mostly, it was, "Oh, gosh. I can't tell you how often I've felt that. How did this Jenny Holzer know?" or, "Look, honey . . . that's a page from my diary."

But it was a dialogue between two New Yorkers that I enjoyed the most. It gave me pause. The woman said, "That's me—absolutely *me*. The first thing I do every morning is worry."

Her companion answered (in this strong Brooklyn brogue), "Ah've told ya not to worry. Why ya worry when ahm wid ya?" They never took their eyes off the vellum, as if it could harbor or analyze their personal confessions. They stood there a long time, contemplating what those lines meant to them personally. And I stayed with them like a little mouse in the corner, just to observe.

WORRYING BASED ON SUSPICION

I love it when something reflects the human condition in such a unique way. That couple could have been any of us. We worry about general things in preparation for the trouble we somehow know will soon come. It's the suspicion upon which we build a case for concern.

Worry is probably a bigger deterrent to freedom than any other emotion. Everybody, to varying degrees, has the capacity to worry: the old, the young, the rich, the poor, the educated, the uneducated, the sick, the well, the employed, the unemployed, the beggar, the king, the believer, and the unbeliever. If you're in the human condition, you have experienced this feeling. I have a friend who worries if she's not worried because she lives on the premise there will always be something to get her down. Since life is not perfect, we have to worry about something. So she looks for it every day.

All the while God says, *Why ya worry when Ahm wid ya?*

Good question. Why *do* we worry when we also have the capacity to trust Him? Because it's human nature. I *want* to take Him at His word, remembering there's no alignment of forces against me, but sometimes I can't. I simply can't! I say to myself in a worrisome situation, *Fahgeddaboudit... He's got ya covered, Luci.* But before trust can get a stronghold in my mind and heart, worry starts.

BIG MAMA WORRY'S OFFSPRING

Well, that's not quite right. To tell you the truth, I'm more of a fretter than a worrier. It's somewhat the same, but fretting is more the offspring of Big Mama Worry— the *child* of Worry. It's younger, smaller, and less grown up than worry, but it produces the same results: no freedom of spirit because it wears me out. Fretting happens when I give in to feelings of irritation, impatience, or petulance. Little things gnaw at my insides, pulling my spirit down. I rarely sit around worrying about the lack of world peace or government spending or the rise and fall of the stock market (although I'd be affected by the negative movement of any of these) because I'm not infected with worrying; I'm infected with fretting.

I started out as a heavy-duty worrier, but something happened when I was twenty-five that changed me. The year was 1956, and I'd taken a job as a traveling representative for the college from which I had graduated the year before. My grandfather had bought me my first car, which enabled me to drive from place to place in Texas,

Oklahoma, and Louisiana, contacting young women to interest them in my alma mater—Mary Hardin Baylor College (MHBC)—and ideally to recruit them.

(At the time MHBC was a women's college but has since become coed and grown to about six times its original size. It's a Christian school in Belton, Texas. Both my mother and my aunt had attended in the 1920s, so I wanted to follow suit. Aunt Ernestine was an art major, which interested me a lot. I admired her a great deal and decided to pursue the same discipline of study . . . but I digress.)

Although the job was very enjoyable, it was also demanding in terms of setting up appointments with potential students and their parents. I often had to spend the night in a hotel or motel between interviews. I'd need to be in one state at ten o'clock one morning, then in another state the next morning. It was on one of these long excursions between states that this particular incident happened.

I was driving over a lengthy stretch of highway one evening about dusk when I began to realize the car behind me was following me. Being a single young woman and alone, I always tried to be very careful, but this car was too close for comfort, and that unnerved me. I could tell the driver was a man, also alone, and I started to worry. I imagined his forcing me off the road, robbing me, harming me, raping me perhaps, and even killing me. The whole scenario played over and over in my head! I tried to ditch him: sped up, turned off on a side road for a mile or two . . . but every attempt was futile. He stuck with me like glue. It was obvious he was following my car. I was absolutely seized by fear and worry.

Because it was late in the day and I still had a lot of miles before my final destination, I decided to pull in at the nearest motel to try to get a greater measure of security behind a locked door. As I registered, I saw the man's car parked with the lights on about half a block away, waiting. So I hurriedly carried my things into the little motel room, immediately bolted the door, and snapped the chain into the slot. When I heard a car pull up in front of that room, I started to cry and pray. I was shaking with worry. Afraid for my life. I can't even tell you how deep the anxiety in my heart rumbled around. It made me sick to my stomach.

I admitted to God that I was scared to death. Worried I might be attacked or killed. I talked to Him about my panic and my insecure feelings. It became a running monologue to God. Talking. Talking. Talking to Him. I asked Him to show Himself in all His power, whatever that meant. I asked for protection and deliverance from this awful fear and the strength to trust Him and not worry. I was completely vulnerable—both to whomever was on the outside of that door and to God. I simply was not in charge.

In return, it was as though God said to me, *Keep moving, Luci. Get ready for bed and trust Me. I'm with you. Don't worry.* At that moment, I stood up and turned toward the center of the room. I remember shaking all over. When I got to the dresser, I noticed a little note under the glass on top. It was in somebody's handwriting, and just as clear as day it read, "Come to Me, all who are weary and heavy laden, and I will give you rest. Signed: Jesus."

Those were the exact words written by someone I will never know. In the quietest, simplest way, God had shown Himself in all His power. His Word!

I could not believe my eyes, and an incredible feeling of strength swept through me. I knew beyond a shadow of a doubt that God was answering my prayer to "show Himself." It really was as though He was standing in front of me, talking to me—strong, powerful, calm, and very direct. That awful dread and fear of attack began to slip away. I actually had peace. I knew God was with me. I got ready for bed and slept like a baby all night long. There was not even a hint of trouble, and the next morning I went to my car, feeling confident that I was safe in God. No stranger was waiting for me, and the questionable car was nowhere to be seen.

For weeks after that, when I was in my car driving, I sang praises to God and thanked Him again and again for His presence, provision, and protection. It meant the world to me, and since that time, I've also known beyond a shadow of a doubt that God will keep His word. When I'm weary and heavy laden, it is He who gives me rest. He says to me over and over, *Don't worry*. There's nothing in the world like freedom from that negative emotion. It's that same principle to which I made reference in chapter 9 when the guy with the rolled-up newspaper was waiting for me outside the Norwalk City Hall. That happened many years later, but it was the same power from God's Spirit at work. At a time like that, when one calls upon God and is able to apply memorized scripture to the situation, it gives a sense of peace. The Word of God somehow floods your being and sets you free from deep worry. I can't explain it. I just know it happens.

FINDING RELEASE FROM WORRY

The apostle Paul addressed this topic in Philippians 4. And he's a good advocate to give us knowledge beyond a shadow of a doubt because when he wrote the book of Philippians, Paul was under house arrest in Rome. He was bound with chains, and he remained that way for two years. Yet he offered these words in the middle of that imprisonment. Look at verses 6–7:

Don't fret or worry. Instead of worrying, pray. Let petitions and praises shape your worries into prayers, letting God know your concerns. Before you know it, a sense of God's wholeness, everything coming together for good, will come and settle you down. It's wonderful what happens when Christ displaces worry at the center of your life. (MSG)

Also, read the first verse of Psalm 46: "God is our refuge and strength, a very present help in trouble" (NKJV). The Hebrew word for *trouble* means "to be restricted, to be tied up in a narrow, cramped place." It implies no freedom. That's what we feel when we're restricted: bound, cramped, in bondage. But when we seek refuge in God, He releases us to move around freely. We're free from fear. Free from stress. Free from worry. I might fret and feel anxiety from time to time, but I know for a fact that God is my Refuge, and nothing can happen to me that He does not permit.

The last verse of Psalm 37 says,

> The spacious, free life is from GOD,
>   it's also protected and safe.
> GOD-strengthened, we're delivered from evil—
>   when we run to him, he saves us. (MSG)

That is precisely what happened that night fifty years ago, and the assurance that it was God who saved me changed me forever. (Again, remember the newspaper-roller and how God protected me from him? He gave me quick responses then got me outta there. He protected me.)

Let me suggest we replace worry with worship. After all, if we're willing to fight for the freedom of worship, we ought to make good use of that freedom, shouldn't we?

A wise person once said, "Every tomorrow has two handles. We can take hold of it by the handle of anxiety or by the handle of faith." Worry never robs tomorrow of its problems; it saps today of its freedom. Worry takes a lot of energy. Try your best not to spend your energy that way.

THAT LITTLE NAGGING VISITOR

But now, *fretting*? I don't know why, but that seems to be another story. It's often my picky, little nagging visitor. I so wish I wouldn't fret. Frankly, I think it's become a bad habit, and I tell myself, *Habits can be broken, Luci.* I've been praying about it, asking God to explain why I do it and to help me not to. It's all related to control issues—I want my way and don't get it; I have to wait in line when I'm out of time; I'm interrupted in the middle of my own plans; I prefer to be with someone other than the person I'm with; I'm prompt, and the other person is late; I don't feel a situation is fair . . . yada yada yada. You name it; I've thought it. This is when I feel those forces aligning quietly and assume there's going to be trouble, not in the Big Mama Worry world of real life, but in the nagging sameness of every day.

All I know to do is to keep committing my life to the Lord, seeking His guidance and direction. I'm asking Him to help me get out of my way and let Him take the lead. I'm also asking Him to make me content no matter where I find myself. A lot of it has to do with being an adult and acting like one. Kids fret. Seems that I should be outgrowing that little petulant way, doesn't it? And because I want to change, I'm trying very hard to do what my dear, wonderful friend Jan Silvious suggests in her fine book *Big Girls Don't Whine: Getting On with the Great Life God Intends.* She writes,

Being a Big Girl is what all those years you lived as a real little girl were about. The lessons you learned, the mistakes you made, the insecurities revealed in you, all make the treasure of the Big Girl inside an incredible find. This treasure allows every Little Girl to experience the freedom God intends for her. It is the freedom to move on from the past to find healthy relationships. It is the freedom to be a confident Big Girl in a whiney Little-Girl world. It is the freedom to experience a life of potential and vision.

The treasure of a Big Girl is available to every Little Girl. This priceless state of being is intended by God for each woman He creates.[1]

Living like this means knowing beyond the shadow of a doubt you're experiencing the true freedom you've been given in Christ and enjoying it.

12

Splurging in God's Abundant Gifts

Claiming and enjoying the intangibles
that are greater than gold

The ancient Greeks had an interesting way of looking at things. They believed that to marvel over something was to have the beginning of knowledge, and when one stopped marveling, the danger of ceasing to know set in.

That's kind of a mental tongue twister, but I think there's truth to it. When something is "marvelous," it causes us to stop and think. To look. To ponder. To wonder. To marvel means to be curious about something. Marveling is full of surprise and amazement. It takes our breath away. And when something evokes these kinds of thoughts and emotions as we marvel at it, we want to know more about why we're amazed in the first place.

By the same token, when we *stop* marveling or wondering, a kind of lethargy and/or indifference begins. We stop asking questions. We don't look as deliberately or quizzically at things. We're not curious anymore. Or we simply don't care. We can even turn cold.

The wonder and marvel of a relationship . . . or a job . . . or a cause . . . can wane when there's no longer relevance that holds our interest. Knowing and caring about the other person cease to excite us, and we become trapped in a way of living that binds us to boredom, lethargy, or worst of all, a prison of our own making.

I'm sad to say that I've known too many people who live their whole lives this way. They simply cannot unlock the chains that bind them to the earth and learn there's a world of wonder out there waiting to be discovered. For believers in Jesus Christ, this is the worst place in the world to be. Not only has the joy of our salvation lost its verve, but we're so out of fellowship with the Savior we can't seem to move forward or backward. We're stuck. And there's nothing worse than being stuck. There's no freedom . . . inside or out. And the truth is, many believers don't even know they're stuck. They just live lives of what Henry David Thoreau called "quiet desperation."

Remember in the book of Revelation when the apostle

John wrote letters to the seven churches centering on things that were taking place at that time? They were real, existing churches that needed either affirmation or confrontation. And John transcribed the Lord's words to these churches in chapters 2 and 3. Note what He says in 3:14–21 when addressing the church in Laodicea. I like the way Eugene Peterson translates it into the language of our day. Remember, the Lord is talking:

> I know you inside and out, and find little to my liking. You're not cold, you're not hot—far better to be either cold or hot! You're stale. You're stagnant. You make me want to vomit. You brag, "I'm rich, I've got it made, I need nothing from anyone," oblivious that in fact you're a pitiful, blind beggar, threadbare and homeless. . . . The people I love, I call to account—prod and correct and guide so that they'll live at their best. Up on your feet, then! About face! Run after God! (MSG)

The church at Laodicea had lost its wonder. The people marveled over nothing. They were "stagnant," and Christ said it made Him want to vomit. These are very strong words! In the last verse of chapter 3, Jesus asks, "Are your ears awake? Listen. Listen to the Wind Words" (v. 21 MSG), referring to the Holy Spirit moving in their midst.

GETTING UNSTUCK FROM BEING STAGNANT

What can make us turn around when we come to our senses and realize we've become stagnant? Is there any hope for us to get free from being stuck there? I believe there is. Peterson's translation suggests two ways: "Run after God!" and "Listen. Listen to the Wind Words." In other words, pursue God in every way you know how and pay attention to what His Holy Spirit is saying to you, albeit ever so quietly and personally.

For myself, although I've not been weighed down by stagnation, I've had ideas that were less than wonderful, and God has had to turn me around and make me run after Him instead of taking the path I originally planned.

For example, it never occurred to me that I'd ever be a speaker in public Christian ministry. Both my brothers were pastor/teachers; my older brother was a missionary in South America for almost forty years. *That's enough for one family*, I thought. But for me to teach or speak? No way! Although I was a strong believer, I loved being in the corporate world, and my plans were to have a career, retire about the age of fifty or fifty-five, travel all over the globe, read books to my heart's content, visit all the art museums in the world, finally settle down in my home where I'd have dinner parties for friends and neighbors, and live a quiet life with no one to bother me or ask of me anything I didn't want to do.

In fact, during the majority of my "business" years, it was to that end that I worked. And I loved it, knowing one day all my dreams would come true. I saved my money for that purpose and worked overtime to bring retirement as early as possible.

One day my friend Ney Bailey asked, "Have you ever thought about speaking, Luci? Or writing books? I think you'd do both beautifully. You have a strong faith and communicate well, and it would be wonderful to hear you speak and to read your thoughts. You write great letters. Why couldn't you also write great books?"

"Absolutely not, Ney," I answered. "I have no desire whatsoever to do either of those, and I can tell you now, that'll never happen. Read my lips: no." Then I told her about all the plans I had for retiring, traveling, reading, and so forth. She didn't bring it up again, but what she didn't know was that her voice became the "Wind Words" to which I listened. Her suggestion would not leave my head. I thought about it all the time. I even prayed about what she asked me to consider. It was the strangest thing. Something about it seemed actually doable, wonderful, and I found myself marveling at the idea. I told no one, but I remember it made me feel energized. This was in 1982.

Amazingly, shortly after that I was invited to speak at a meeting in Oregon for Multnomah Press, and following a bit of pondering and praying, I accepted and went

to that meeting with fear and trembling. Just before I
left, Ney gave me a little plaque that read,

> Then the LORD stretched out His hand and touched
> my mouth, and the LORD said to me, *Behold, I have
> put my words in your mouth. . . .*
>
> Jeremiah 1:9

> I love you, Luci . . . you're going to be great.
>
> Ney

That little plaque hangs on my wall today, and each
time I look at it, I marvel.

Countless doors have opened for me to marvel at
God's ways of changing my stagnant ideas into those
that pulsate with His plans. And once I started speaking
and writing, I began traveling all over the world . . . vis-
iting art museums on every continent. And now, I not
only read the books I want to but also have built a
library in my house for them; I can walk into the next
room and pull them off my shelves. I have dinner parties for friends and neighbors in a house I built and dedi-
cated to Him. I surprise myself every day that I'm in this
place, enjoying the wonder of it all, by God's grace. And
quite frankly, the wonder of it all flows from the ministry God has opened to me, the people I've met, the
team of which I am a part, and the joy of being involved

in helping people understand the wonderful grace of God.

TOTALLY AND COMPLETELY DEPRAVED

One of the most recent marvels happened in 2004 when Mary Graham asked me to give the gospel the following year as a part of my presentation at Women of Faith conferences. Being a slow learner, I told Mary the same thing I'd said to Ney: "Absolutely not, Mary. Read my lips: no."

I was nervous that I might not do it well. I had shared my faith with various people through the years . . . friends, acquaintances . . . but the thought of being responsible for presenting it to thousands of strangers made me feel very uncomfortable. I simply didn't want to. I didn't know enough, and I certainly didn't feel confident enough to go up on that platform and represent the Lord in that manner. Since I believe the greatest and most important decision one can make in life is to be rightly related to God, I felt totally inadequate for explaining that process. But Mary insisted and set it in motion to begin in the 2005 conferences.

As the first conference of the year drew near, I felt immobilized but didn't want to whine about it or make it a bigger deal than it was, so I just fretted silently.

(Remember, I'm good at that!) The presentation of the gospel is one of the most important parts of the weekend for us. We've learned through the years that many of the women who attend are seeking personal faith, but they don't know how to begin a relationship with God. Many others have little or no interest in matters of faith, but they become interested during the conference. In a room the size of an arena, we find there are always hundreds who respond to an invitation to know Christ if we simply tell them how they can. But did I want to be the one to tell them? Well . . . no! And . . . yes!

One day I decided to call my brother Chuck to see if he and I could have lunch together in order for me to dump my fear on him and get his counsel. I just knew he'd say, "Well, of course, you don't have to give the gospel, Sis. If you're not comfortable, there's no way Mary can force you to do it." Mary and Chuck are very good friends, and I knew he'd be able to reason her out of her determination if I couldn't.

Before that meeting I typed out a long list of questions to ask Chuck and went armed with those as well as all my excuses and fears. This was January 11, 2005. The minute I walked in the door of the restaurant and told Chuck what I was feeling and that I simply wasn't qualified to do what Mary wanted, he said, "Sis, this is the most wonderful thing you could be invited to do. You have the opportunity to tell people the greatest news in the world. What a gift Mary has given you. I'm so proud of you!"

Shoot. There went all my defenses, so I laid my fears aside and started asking questions instead:

LUCI: After accepting Christ as Savior by faith, what are the most important ingredients a person needs to live a life of faith?

CHUCK: Make sure the new Christian has *assurance* that God will do what He says. Refer to 1 John 5:11–12. It's all about *life*. God said it, we believe it, and He'll do what He says. Second, we need faith when it comes to *prayer*. Relate the new believer to God the Father—ask, seek, knock. Third, the believer is *forgiven*. Don't keep dragging your sin around. It's been forgiven. And finally, God is *sovereign*. Even when we can't explain why, God doesn't make a mistake with our lives. See Daniel 4:35.

LUCI: What do you remember from our childhood about how we understood faith being important for the whole of life?

CHUCK: The experience of going through World War II taught us as a family to trust God. As children we had lots of questions, which we asked Mother and Daddy. They prayed with us and asked God to protect us. It was Mother and Orville [our older brother], though, who had unbelievable faith in the family. Mother was like a steer in the wind . . . unmovable! And Orville's behavior and response to trials were a huge symbol to me that God could be trusted to meet our needs.

LUCI: What do you think are the hardest situations for most people to demonstrate faith?

CHUCK: It's a toss-up between several things: *Finances*— when you feel responsible, you worry about whether or not you're going to be able to make ends meet. It's also a combination of *health issues—aging and dying.* I'd tie all of these together as a very hard spot to demonstrate faith, and as we get older, they become harder to manage. There's a constant need to apply faith in all these areas. I also seem to always have the feeling I'm going to forget things . . . get Alzheimer's or lose my mind. I couldn't function if I couldn't remember things. Wouldn't that be awful, Sis? I rely a lot on my memory of what I know—or used to know, if I can just remember it.

LUCI: What basic principles do you apply when you give the gospel message to somebody? Do you use the same principles with everybody?

CHUCK: OK, first, I *assume the hearer has no clue what I'm talking about.* Lots of people think they're Christians because their parents are or because they pay their taxes or some such thing. So just start by talking like they don't know anything about your subject. You have good news, and you want to tell them about it.

Second, I *talk to them like they're children*. I use word pictures. Keep your points very simple. No big words or confusing thoughts. The gospel is basically very simple. It's simple truth that, when heeded, can change a life. Third, I *assume the hearers want to know what I have to say*. I'm excited about the gift I want to give them, and I want them to get excited too. If they don't know about the gift . . . they don't know they don't. And fourth, I *treat everyone with respect*. I never want the hearer to feel insulted. Always be respectful of your listener. If they talk or ask questions, listen to what they have to say.

Our visit went on for three hours. It was one of the most enjoyable times I ever had with my brother. We laughed a lot, relived happenings in our childhood, reminisced about old times, and even cried a bit. It was very sweet and meaningful and encouraging to me as I was about to take on a new project in which I had much more fear than wonder. In the end, I asked Chuck how he would give the gospel, were he in my shoes. He said, "Salvation is a gift, Sis. It's God's greatest gift to humankind. Make that very clear. We were all born separated from God, but God made provision for that separation by having His Son die for my sins. In Ephesians 2:8, Eugene Peterson says, 'Saving is all [God's] idea, and all his work. All we do is trust him enough to let him do it. It's God's gift from start to finish!' [MSG]. Grace is receiving what we don't deserve, cannot earn, and are unable to repay. Romans 3 says, 'All have sinned, and come short of the glory of God,' and Romans 6 says, 'The wages of sin is death; but the gift of God is eternal life through Jesus Christ our Lord' [KJV]. With Christ's death, the penalty for sin was paid in full. Give the listener an opportunity to accept Christ as their Savior. Say a simple prayer, and suggest they repeat it with you, in their heart."

When we got ready to leave, Chuck said this final thing that I thought was so fabulous: "Sis, we are all depraved. Humanity is depraved. Check out Isaiah 53:6, where it talks about all of us being like sheep going astray. If depravity were blue, we'd be blue all over. Throughout! If you cut us, everything inside would be blue, just as everything outside is blue. We are totally and completely depraved. This is why we need a sinless, harmless, totally pure Savior. And this is who we have in Jesus Christ."

IN AWE AND WONDER

By the time we finished that lunch and visit, my fears were gone. I was walking on air. I could have killed giants. I was in awe and wonder at the abundance of God's gifts and provisions. I was even looking forward to giving the gospel during the upcoming 2005 conferences, and I still enjoy doing it week after week. The thing I thought I'd dislike the most has become the most enjoyable part of the whole weekend for me.

We see so many women come to Women of Faith conferences who don't understand that God has a plan for their lives to give them hope. They feel defeated and abandoned by everybody . . . especially God. Many come depressed, having been misunderstood or abused. They have no idea that God loves them, supplies all their needs, and showers them with grace and forgiveness.

On Saturday afternoon when the gospel is given, it's the highlight of the entire conference because that's the moment when these women are given a quiet, thoughtful opportunity to put their faith in the Savior. It's their moment to leave the bondage of sin and walk into freedom—freedom on the inside and freedom on the outside—based on God's marvelous promise:

I know what I'm doing. I have it all planned out— plans to take care of you, not abandon you, plans to give you the future you hope for. (Jeremiah 29:11 MSG)

PART 3

Free to Express Yourself

Marilyn Meberg and
Luci Swindoll

13

Marilyn Asks, "What Does Freedom Mean to You, Luci?"

MARILYN: *First of all, define freedom for me, Luci, and tell me what you experience when you feel really free.*

LUCI: Freedom is the ability to determine one's own actions, to have no confinement or restrictions . . . to be at liberty. When I'm doing something creative, I feel very free, like making something with my hands or writing for my own enjoyment with no deadline or pressure to perform. It's the ability to have independence without constriction. And spiritually speaking, I feel free when there's no threat of legalism . . . when no one is imposing their rules or spirit of correction on me.

MARILYN: *Can you think of a time as a little girl when you felt completely free? What were the circumstances?*

LUCI: I remember loving to draw, or coloring in my coloring books, or playing baseball, running outside, jumping, playing "kick the can." I felt total independence, no restriction. I could be me. I wasn't being told what to do. I loved that. Even to this day, I hate being told what to do. It's one of my pet peeves.

MARILYN: *What do you think causes people to lose that sense of freedom they had in childhood?*

LUCI: It's a combination of things: growing up and becoming an adult, taking on responsibilities, being too serious about life, forgetting that child-spirit inside, no sense of playfulness. We get caught in the fast lane of activities and tend to live there, forgetting how to celebrate, forgetting how to let our hair down and enjoy life. I believe we have to want to be free or it's very easy to let ourselves be bound by tradition, protocol, other people's demands, feelings, and restrictions. I'm not talking about "breaking laws" to be free; I'm talking about having an inner spirit that looks for one's own expression and way of life apart from what society dictates.

MARILYN: *What do you tell the woman who wakes up with sixteen things to do but wants to be free?*

LUCI: Well, I can give her a list. Academically, I can say, "Count your blessings. Learn to tell the difference between inconveniences and catastrophes. Savor the moment. Look for the funny side of life." All these ideas are good things to remember. I'd also tell her that freedom is a choice. Quite often, it's not so much *behavior* as it is an *attitude*. This is where a spiritual life of faith and trust is so important, I think. That woman may be up to her ears in an insurmountable amount of duties as a wife and mother, but within all that, there's freedom in knowing Christ. He has given her promises that tell her she's not alone; He is with her to help her carry her burden. When she accepts that, believes it, and applies it to those sixteen things she's doing, they somehow don't feel so awful. I also think it's important for her to remember that everything has *come to pass*. Those sixteen things that are driving her crazy now won't last forever. They have a shelf life. Everything has a shelf life. So I'd say, "Enjoy what you can and give the rest to God to handle."

MARILYN: *Do you think people are free but don't know it?*
LUCI: Oh yes. Absolutely. And that's terribly sad, I think. When people come to know the Lord, when they accept Christ as their Savior and pray to receive Him, they have been at that moment set free—and by that act of faith alone, they're free to experience

another way of life. But unfortunately, until they are taught that truth from Scripture, they remain spiritually bound, for the rest of their life in some cases. I've known people like this. I want to take them by the shoulders and say, "You don't have to live this way. You have a million promises from God right at your fingertips that will lift you out of the shoulds and oughts and musts. But you're living like you're in a dark prison. You've got the key to open the prison door. Do it. Step out into the sunshine." It goes back to that thing of having to *want* to be free before you can find freedom. Christ is the key, but walking out of the prison door is up to the individual.

MARILYN: *Have you ever started out feeling free and somehow, in the mishmash of life, that sense of freedom was taken from you . . . like a thief came along and stole it?*

LUCI: Yes. I've felt free, but freedom can be short-lived, I think. It has to be "re-won," so to speak. There are a jillion things in daily life that can rob us of our freedom. For example, when I've been praying about something very sincerely, wanting something corrected in me, or when I have seen something I've fretted about or been concerned about, I've raised my head from that prayer and felt tremendous freedom, knowing, *That problem's not even mine anymore.*

I gave it to God. But then, the very next day, I'll drag it back up again and start being concerned for the same old reasons.

MARILYN: *Why do you think that happens?*

LUCI: Reality sets in. I look at my circumstances instead of the fact that God has told me He is taking care of that problem. I forget about my prayer and start working on this really elaborate way of "getting out" of my dilemma instead of leaving it with God, as I was doing yesterday. Human nature. I can think of lots of reasons it happens.

MARILYN: *What is it about freedom that we thwart when we know we can have it all the time? What do we do to stop that process?*

Luci: We don't let go. We don't let go of our worries; we don't let go of our desires, our plans, our possessions, our friends, our families. The list goes on and on! We want to control. Even though I think of myself as relatively free, I can easily get in the way of what God is trying to teach me because I think my plans are better. He has to keep showing me that He's in charge and I'm not. I'm in my seventies and still learning that lesson. Will there ever be a time I get it and stop wanting my way? I wonder!

MARILYN: *Luci, who's the freest person you've ever known?*

LUCI: One of the freest persons I've known personally is my brother Chuck. I know some of the things he has overcome, I know his pathology, I know his history, I know his scholarly bent for learning the truth about the Bible, and I know what he teaches. I know that he lives out of who he really is and what he knows for sure. And out of that, I see a man who is spiritually free.

MARILYN: *Why do you think he's as free as he is?*

LUCI: He understands the grace of God. He not only understands it; he embraces it and lives out of it. He copes with his life out of those teachings and the truth of grace.

MARILYN: *Do you think he feels that?*

LUCI: I've never asked him that question, but he probably does. I think he knows what to do with problems or troublesome issues in his life. He knows to let go; he knows to keep giving them to the Lord; he knows to pray. He's got all of the accoutrements it takes to be free. Besides that, he was raised in a family in which all of us could express our freedom. We could say what we thought without being put down.

MARILYN: *Do you think he is free in a way he has always been free, or can you see the progression of freedom's impact?*

LUCI: The more he knows about the Bible, the freer he becomes, I believe, because when one compares everything under the Mosaic Law and what it taught and the good it did to what we have now in Christ, there's an enormous impact of freedom. We are new creations, and Chuck knows it from the original language (all the nuances and ramifications), and he lives out of it. He's not perfect, of course, but I think he's pretty close. *[Smile.]* He's perfect in Christ. In his problem areas, he really seeks to find what is the best and truest way to handle those problems and the most expedient way to live a grace-filled life. I really respect that in him . . . and in anyone!

MARILYN: *Without mentioning names, do you know anybody who shares your faith and who is not free?*

LUCI: Oh yeah. I have Christian friends who aren't free because they don't understand the grace of God. They think they have to perform to stay in God's favor or God will quit loving them.

MARILYN: *How can you enhance or accelerate or cooperate with the process of being free?*

LUCI: In my view, the acceleration of the process—if it can be called that—is the degree to which you as a person abide in Christ. Ask yourself the question, "How deeply do I want to know Christ?" If I want to honor Him, if I want to please Him, that's going to take human effort by agreeing with what God wants to do with my life. And it means overcoming. It means facing those things that are hard for me or seem impossible and saying, "By golly, I'll do it. I *will* keep going. I *will* do the next thing." For instance, people talk about how impossible it is to be a "Proverbs 31 woman," but I think that passage means simply doing the next thing. If you take life one step at a time, it's what we do every day. It's possible to do the next thing, which is the only way to face anything. There are ways we can either thwart or accelerate freedom. It depends a lot on how much we really and truly want it for ourselves.

MARILYN: *How does a person who is in Christ learn to experience freedom?*

LUCI: You have to have biblical teaching that is sound. If you study under someone who is a good Bible teacher and ask the Spirit to open your heart to what is being taught, you will grow. It's like being in school. As you go from the sixth grade to the twelfth grade, you pay attention, you study, you read, you apply yourself, you use your head and engage your heart, and you grow. You won't suddenly be an adult. But you can graduate. You will know something. You may not know a lot, but certainly more than you did when you started. The more you study, apply, try things, the more you grow. It's a logical progression, and when you depend on God's Spirit, it becomes sort of *theo*logical. You grow up in your life and in Christ, as well.

MARILYN: *Do you think it's easier for a person who experiences freedom to give it to others?*

LUCI: Absolutely! My premise is this: you cannot give what you don't have. You can't give the money you don't have, you can't give the time you don't have, you can't give the energy you don't have, and you certainly can't give freedom to somebody if you don't even know you have it. Freedom is a wonderful thing to teach to others, but I never learned anything about it except from people who were free themselves. And the best way to give it is to model it.

MARILYN: *Luci, you seem to be very free. But some women could never be happy if they were not married. That would never be a freedom lifestyle for them. To what do you attribute your freedom as a single person?*

LUCI: I don't think anybody's a whole person until she can define herself without somebody else in the definition. I am my brother's sister, for example. My brother is very famous and very well loved and respected, and that's great, but I am me, and he is himself. His persona and attributes don't splash over on me just because I'm a Swindoll. I believe the only way you can enjoy freedom, married or single, is to know yourself, like yourself, and be yourself. And better still, if you can learn to predict patterns and trends in your life, I think you'll experience even more freedom. So whether you're married or single doesn't dictate your freedom. Freedom starts within oneself. The greatest freedom in the world is knowing Christ in a personal way, and when you do, He enables you to know who you are.

Many years ago I asked myself this question: is it more important for me to know me or for me to know Christ? I thought it was more important for me to know me because when I found out about me, I saw this inordinate need of Him. I began to know I had this need and that need, and nobody else was able to meet those needs except God through His Son, Jesus Christ. But when I began to learn more and more about me (my patterns, pride, wants and needs, idiosyncrasies, yearnings, desires, hopes, and fears . . . all that), I could finally define me without somebody else in that definition—a husband, a child, a sibling, a parent, or a friend. That was very important to me, and it was the beginning of my growing up and finding true freedom as a person.

MARILYN: *Does living in freedom mean one is spiritually mature?*

LUCI: That's a good question, Marilyn, but it's kind of tricky to answer. Certainly when one is spiritually mature, she will live in freedom, as I pointed out earlier when I talked about my brother Chuck. The more mature he became in his walk with Christ, the more freedom he enjoyed. The deeper the maturity, the greater the freedom. That's true for anyone! I also think it's possible to have a small measure of freedom without necessarily being spiritually mature. A person can enjoy a certain level of fellowship with the Lord but be young in her faith. You can enjoy enough freedom to make sound decisions, have peace, joy, sweet fellowship, love, . . . but not necessarily be what I would call "grown up" in Christ. The truth is, we can live in bits and pieces of freedom for a long time, knowing we're free, but the more mature we become in Christ, the more freedom we experience on all levels.

MARILYN: *You talk a lot about financial freedom and the freedom to give. You've had a very successful professional career. Now you're an author and a speaker, and you're well established financially. How can someone* *who does not have that financial security have the freedom to give?*

LUCI: Start with the idea that everything you have is a gift from God. The very breath you breathe is God's gift to you. The money you make, the home you have, whatever you have, it's God's gift. Out of the knowledge that it's all a gift, you give. You start where you are, and you learn to share what you have and give what God puts on your heart. I believe that giving grows. I was taught to give when I was a little girl, and through the years I've learned to give more and more. I personally feel freer when I give. I'm not wealthy, but in Christ I'm a millionaire. So I try to give accordingly—even sacrificially at times—and I think anybody can give out of that kind of spirit if they really want to.

MARILYN: *Consider this scenario: A woman does not like to go to church, so she stops. She does not like to read the Bible, so she does not read the Bible. She falls asleep when she prays, so she decides not to pray. She hates her job, so she quits. Is she free?*

LUCI: It's a pseudosense of freedom. She's not truly free because she's not responsible, and if she continues like that, she'll wind up an ignorant, unbelieving reprobate living in the poorhouse. But hey! The choice is hers. I think we're responsible for our own lives, for our own mental health, for our own well-being, because we're adults. When people hear me speak on the Women of Faith stage, they might think, *She's always been like this—established, centered, content, squared-away*—but I haven't. I've learned the hard way what to say no to. I've learned when to accept things and when not to. We learn after a period of time that true freedom is when we accept who we are, we try to help other people, we give our lives away to the degree we can, we're a servant to others, we try to teach what God is teaching us, and we want to make a difference. We learn boundaries and responsibilities A lot of responsibility comes with true freedom.

MARILYN: *Do you believe that the more you understand your own freedom the more you're able to give freedom?*
LUCI: Absolutely! As I said earlier, we can only give what we have, and the more I understand what I have, the more I want to share it with others.

MARILYN: *Luci, have you ever been in a relationship that was very important to you and you wanted to control someone you loved? In your heart you thought it was good for the person to do what you wanted, but they simply wouldn't. Let's say you had the power to impede that person's freedom . . . would you do that to get what you wanted?*

LUCI: Let me answer that this way: I think there's not a person on earth who has not felt that and probably done that. It's human nature to want to control someone we love or love to be with (even though we wouldn't call it control, necessarily). We want the person to do what we want. Especially when we're young and inexperienced and think we know everything in the world. And if the person doesn't do what we want, we try to find a way to help him or her come to that conclusion. I've had friends I've wanted to do that to, or I've even had bosses I wished would see things my way because I thought I was right. I've even wanted that with God: would He just see things my way? Could I just write a little postscript on the document He sends me so He'll see I have a better idea than His?

MARILYN: *How did that part of your nature change?*

LUCI: In that year or so when I got to know me—my tendencies, patterns, idiosyncrasies—I began to see ways I was controlling others, and I hated it in myself. When I went to bed at the end of the day, I would think of how I had interacted with others. I'd ask myself, *What are you achieving, Luci? What will you have when they do what you want? When they read what you want them to read, when they behave as you want them to behave? You'll have a clone. Do you want that? The whole reason you like them now is that they're themselves ... and not you.* I began to see I was trying to create another me, and I was having enough trouble living with me as it was! As I saw these patterns develop, I thought about it and prayed about it and really addressed it in myself. I thought, *Sometimes I just can't be with them because I'm going to control them,* and I hated that. I was sick of me! I was sick of my own controlling voice. So I set about trying to change. I still work at it and probably always will. I pray about it a lot, asking God to help me continually let go. As my mother used to say, "It takes a lifetime to learn how to live."

MARILYN: *One final question. Winston Churchill said, "The soul of freedom is deathless; it cannot and will not perish." What does that mean to you personally?*

LUCI: It means when a person is free inside and out, there's no stopping her. Because we were created to be free eternally, that is a "deathless truth," so to speak. Freedom cannot die! For me personally, it means to keep striving for freedom and enjoying the many gifts that come with it. Christ has set me free, and that's the best news in the world. I think it's the only way to live a full life and bring honor to the Lord.

14

Luci Asks, "What Does Freedom Mean to You, Marilyn?"

LUCI: *Marilyn, explain the difference between freedom and discipline.*

MARILYN: Freedom, I think, is inherent in the human spirit. We were born for freedom, so we quest for it. Discipline can be from outside or inside ourselves because we learn that without discipline there are consequences. That lesson can inhibit our freedoms.

LUCI: *Don't you think freedom without responsibility is one of the worst things in the world? If you're free to do anything you want with anyone, that can lead to personal chaos.*

MARILYN: Absolutely, but that freedom is separate from discipline. If I have freedom but I have no discipline, I create an environment of chaos.

LUCI: *Do you think anybody prefers bondage?*
MARILYN: Yes. It's much safer. I think many people prefer bondage.

LUCI: **And why is it safe?**
MARILYN: Because it's known. The restrictions are known. The parameters are defined. They're observable; they're tangible.

LUCI: *Don't you think women who have been dominated by their husbands may then feel they don't deserve any freedom? They think,* This shouldn't be mine?
MARILYN: You won't think, *I shouldn't,* unless something has prepared you in your mind or your spirit to think, *I don't deserve.* So you bring that mind-set into a marriage. Dominance is never healthy, but to those who have been abused, domination is familiar, and some think it is deserved.

LUCI: *Do you think a bad marriage is the hardest thing in the world?*
MARILYN: I think bad relatedness is the hardest thing in the world.

LUCI: *You become a Christian, you receive Christ, then there's a growth period. Do you believe you can have some measure of control in how you grow?*

MARILYN: Solomon answered that question. In Ecclesiastes 7:29 Solomon said, "God made mankind upright, but men have gone in search of many schemes." So there you have the free-will issue, and that goes back to the original freedom of choice God gave us.

LUCI: *What causes people to be controlling of others?*

MARILYN: If you're insecure, you have to control. Controlling gives the illusion of security.

LUCI: *We all know people who find themselves in absolutely desperate situations, perhaps financially or relationally. They think,* How do I get out of this? How do I free myself from this? *How is freedom expressed in a situation that is so overwhelming? How do you respond to a person whose need is that desperate?*

MARILYN: We remember first of all that God does not call us to bondage but to freedom. That freedom is within. It provides security. It provides assurance that God makes all things work together for good. That does not mean all things *are* good; it means God uses all things for our growth and development internally. Good comes from that development. So that's the inside stuff. The outside stuff in handling a desperate situation is to get outside help: professional counseling, professional money-management advice, or if the kids are derailing, perhaps parenting classes could be illuminating to help understand kid behavior.

LUCI: *What if I'm married to someone whose mother wants to absolutely control our lives, how we spend our money, how we rear our children, and what kind of house we live in? What if I have no freedom because of my husband's mother?*

MARILYN: The husband should not put up with this. He hasn't separated from Mama, so he's got some issues there that create a marital problem. The husband needs to work toward maturing so he can take a stand for his wife instead of passively accepting his mother's domination.

LUCI: *What if I want to be free, but I keep making choices that get me in trouble? Let's say I'm in a relationship—not a sexual relationship, but a very personal relationship with a man at my place of work—and my husband would leave me if he knew how much I cared about the other man and the strong connectedness we have? If I leave my job, I lose one of the most meaningful relationships I've ever had in my life. But if I don't, I'll probably lose my marriage. I feel so trapped I can't even think about freedom.*

MARILYN: You'd better start thinking about right behavior! You're heading for a living hell if you don't get out of that so-called friendship. You say it's not sexual, and maybe you're not acting it out, but that dynamic is there. In time it may cause you to leave your marriage, your children, and your reputation. It may cost you your job. Think about the price you may pay. You've got the freedom now to make good choices. Right now you're heading for a bad choice and its consequences.

LUCI: *What about this scenario, Marilyn? What do you say to the woman who is single but burdened by tremendous debt? She has several credit cards that are maxed out, so she can only pay the minimum every month. She just bought a fancy car she can't afford. She says she does not feel free.*

MARILYN: She's right. She is not free because she's being dominated by purchases used to distract her from her circumstances, in this case, buying and then buying more. She needs to ask herself, *What am I trying to avoid? What's the feeling I don't want to feel? What's the experience I don't want to know about? What's the old wound I want to keep covering up?* She's covering up something with a substitute: buying stuff. She'll never be free until she comes to terms with what's motivating her behavior and then changing her behavior.

LUCI: *Let's say I was raised by a very authoritative father. I would never want my children to go through what I went through. I do not want to quench their spirits, so I let them have all the freedom in the world, and all my friends dislike my children because of their bad behavior. But I'm not going to be telling those kids they can't be free.*

MARILYN: How do you define that freedom?

LUCI: *Just letting the kids make their own choices and be free to grow and experience life.*

MARILYN: How are they doing that? Are they having a good time?

LUCI: *They seem to be having a pretty good time. Do you think I should be more legalistic with my children?*

MARILYN: I don't think the word *legalistic* has anything to do with it. I think you need to give your children boundaries and give them a sense of freedom in knowing what's expected within those boundaries. You are creating insecurity in your children because no child wants to be in charge, in spite of his or her efforts to take control. You've let your children be in charge. You've allowed them to be in charge in response to your growing up with a dad who was autocratic. You are doing them the same degree of disservice your father did to you. It's just on the other end of the spectrum. My suggestion would be that you deal with your own woundedness. Obviously, the fact that your dad was so autocratic has left you with wounds, but you are creating problems now with your children. I suggest parenting classes in an effort to learn some practical skills. And I also would recommend personal therapy for your past hurts.

LUCI: *What is your counsel to a woman whose husband routinely or regularly makes mistakes and it really does impact the freedom of the family?*

MARILYN: The husband and wife have to come together as one. The husband has no right to make decisions without consulting her, nor does she have that right. You are now in a partnership, and you operate as partners. Each has to discuss the pros and cons of a decision, then they together decide what is in the best interests of the family.

LUCI: *As a mother, Marilyn, how do you know when to allow freedom for your children?*

MARILYN: You raise your children on the unshakable foundation of truth, which we learn in Scripture, and you do the best you can to teach that. As they get older, they're going to test it. What do you do? You consistently teach them there's a consequence for misbehavior and disobedience. But ultimately you reach a stage when they're no longer under your authority. You have to let it go then. As a parent, you do everything you can to keep them from derailing. But ultimately if they're going to derail, they're going to derail. That's part of being human. It's also part of growing up. Consequences are great teachers.

LUCI: *Do most kids derail?*

MARILYN: Yes, they do. But I would rather see a young person test boundaries than wait until a midlife crisis causes the derailing years later. By then a marriage and kids can be affected.

LUCI: *Do you think some people have a temperament that is more inclined to seek freedom than others?*

MARILYN: I think some people are more docile in their natures than others. Those people may not quest for freedom with the same vigor and determination as those whose temperaments are inclined to more energetic seeking. I think all temperaments have an inherent drive for freedom, but not all would be willing to give their lives for it.

LUCI: *Did we lose our freedom in the Garden of Eden?*

MARILYN: The freedom to choose good or evil was a part of the Eden environment. God made it clear to the first people on earth that disobedience to His command would result in death. They used their God-given freedom to disobey. When they did, the consequence of sin destroyed perfection, but it did not destroy the freedom to make choices. They— we, all of creation—still have the freedom to make good or bad choices. God did not take that from us. If He had, we'd all be little robots responding to a preprogrammed response. He encourages a good use of our freedom through His Holy Spirit speaking to our spirit. When we listen and use our freedom wisely, our lives reflect order and internal peace.

LUCI: *If you had to recommend one book in the Bible to really understand freedom in Christ, what would that be?*

MARILYN: I recommend the book of Galatians. It teaches the basic and liberating truth of freedom found in knowing Christ personally. In Eugene Peterson's introduction to Galatians in *The Message*, he says, "God is a personal Savior who sets us free to live a free life. God did not coerce us from without, but set us free from within."

LUCI: *If someone said to you, "I want to be freer," what would you suggest that person do?*

MARILYN: In addition to a leisurely walk through Galatians, we all need to continually study the doctrine of grace.

LUCI: *In addition to Scripture, is there a book about freedom that has been especially helpful to you?*

MARILYN: Yes: *Chosen But Free* by Norman Geisler. I dip frequently into this book because of its balanced study of God's sovereignty and our God-given freedom to make human choices. Those choices can be harmful to us or helpful to us. But over and above our option to choose is God's promise to work things for our good. That is His sovereign intention now, and it has been so since before the foundation of the world. I trust Dr. Geisler's scholarship and his clear-headed thinking.

LUCI: *Do you need help with clear-headed thinking, Marilyn?*

MARILYN: I know it comes as a surprise to you, my friend of thirty-four years, but sometimes I need to be reined in.

LUCI: *Well, now you've got my attention! I was on the verge of getting bored. How do you need to be reined in—anything the world may find interesting?*

MARILYN: I saw that glint in your eye, and I also saw you teetering on the verge of boredom. But here's what I mean about being reined in: I'm not talking about my behavior here as much as I'm talking about my thinking. (I noticed your glint disappear.)

LUCI: *So, OK, my glint is gone, and I guess your need to be reined in is not going to reveal juicy tidbits, but I'm still interested about what in you needs reining in.*

MARILYN: I need to be reminded of a fact that gives me much freedom as well as relief. That fact is God does everything He plans to do. Isaiah 14:24, 27 states, "The LORD Almighty has sworn, 'Surely, as I have planned, so it will be, and as I have purposed, so it will stand. . . . For the Lord Almighty has purposed, and who can thwart him? His hand is stretched out, and who can turn it back?" And Isaiah 46:9–11 says, "I am God, and there is no other; I am God, and there is none like me. . . . My purpose will stand, and I will do all that I please. . . . What I have said, that will I bring about; what I have planned, that will I do." So with the freedom and relief I feel that nothing stops God's plans, I need reining in to remember nothing God does requires me. I can become overly conscientious and as a result overcommit myself. I don't need to do that. Why? He does not need me. Instead, He chooses to allow me the privilege of participating in executing His plan. Those reminders about God's sovereign plans not only rein me in, they calm me down. How gracious of God to include me and honor my efforts, but at the same time how freeing to know the success of God's plans is not dependent upon me.

LUCI: *If you could change anything in your life, what would you change?*

MARILYN: Oh, baby, there are many things I would do differently. I would like to think I'd be a less-hurried mother. I have zero recollection of having changed the world because I was always busy doing stuff. But I have many recollections of my children's faces as I sped by them. I did not allow myself freedom from scheduling and enough freedom for mothering.

LUCI: *But I want to know if you'd change any specific experience in your life. Would you have married Ken if you had it to do all over again?*

MARILYN: Well, yes, Barbara Walters, I would marry Ken if I had it to do all over again! But I didn't want to marry him when I accepted his proposal and the sweet diamond ring we picked out at Rivkins Jewelers in Seattle. The closer the wedding date came, the more terrified I became. Finally, my fear was so great I canceled the wedding and gave the ring back.

LUCI: *What was your problem? Why did you say you'd marry him if you didn't want to?*

MARILYN: At the time I wasn't sure what my problem was, but gradually I realized I didn't want to get married, period. I thought I'd lose my freedom. I didn't want to lose my last name (Ricker). I didn't want to sit, stay, or stand on demand. I feared marriage represented a loss of identity and personal freedom. One would think with all those fears I'd been raised in a concentration camp with a barbed-wire fence meant to keep my mother in confinement! But that was not how I saw my parents' marriage, although there *were* times when I thought my mother should "stand" when she didn't. On the other hand, there were many times when she *did* stand. That was encouraging.

LUCI: *So you feared marriage was confinement and not freedom?*

MARILYN: Exactly. As Ken and I talked about my fears, he came to realize it was not that I did not love him. It was that I was scared I'd be a lousy wife. He then made a deal with me and told me if he wanted someone who would sit, stay, or stand, he'd get a cocker spaniel! Ken's mom became a widow when she was only thirty-four years old, and Ken had seen her determination to take hold of life, deal with hard circumstances, and live independently. He was impressed with that.

In fact, he said those qualities were what he'd looked for in a future bride (whomever that might turn out to be). He wanted a "winner and not a clinger." I liked that, agreed to the terms, and got married—and we ultimately had three cocker spaniels. We also reared two wonderful children. But, Luci, here's what I did not know about freedom then: freedom is totally an inside job. It is not about external circumstances. I could be married or single and still not experience freedom.

LUCI: *I hear what you're saying, Marilyn, but what about the woman who is miserable in her marriage and dying to get out of it? Isn't it a stretch to say she's got freedom? I think a miserable marriage sounds like bondage.*

MARILYN: Throughout this book, Luci, we have been saying freedom is an inside job. That is true even in a miserable marriage. It is true in all situations and all circumstances. But if the woman in the miserable marriage is aware of her freedom and determined to live out of her freedom, she will take steps toward fixing her marriage. The free woman knows she does not deserve abuse of any kind on any level. If the partner refuses to change behavior and grow into a loving mate, she may need to separate. Husbands need to learn that loving a wife requires loving her as Christ loves His church. That means the husband considers his wife's needs even ahead of his own. If he wants a blueprint in how to love his wife, he needs to study Jesus. He set a perfect example.

LUCI: *Have you had an experience when you did not allow yourself to have inside freedom?*

MARILYN: There have been many times. For example, when I close down my emotions so I don't feel something I don't want to feel, I have lost my inner freedom. My feelings can no longer flow. It's almost like having a blood clot. That blood cannot flow freely if there's a blood clot. Refusing my emotions the freedom to flow clots me up. Sorry, Luci, this is an unattractive simile; it just occurred to me as we're talking. I'll give you an example of a specific time I shut off my emotions. I'll stop talking about blood.

When our baby Joani was born with spina bifida, I was not allowed to hold her or even touch her. The doctor and nurses warned me I could contaminate the open wound at the base of her spine. It killed me to just stare at her in her little Plexiglas "cage" with one set of armholes in it. I was not allowed to stroke her, touch her little head covered in luxurious black curls, or even caress her tiny toes. Except for the ghastly open wound in her spine, she was a perfectly formed, utterly beautiful baby.

Within a week, Joani developed spinal meningitis

accompanied by a raging fever. She was transferred to another hospital by ambulance, and I was allowed to ride in the back next to her in her isolette. There was no nurse present. I was overwhelmed with the desire to just touch her. I gingerly placed my right hand into the armhole of the isolette. I lightly stroked her perfect little head and then her tiny little shoulders with my forefinger. She was my flesh and blood, bone of my bone, flesh of my flesh. I pulled my arm out then and sobbed, "Lord Jesus, heal her! Please heal her!" My emotions at that moment nearly drowned me. I did not think I could contain or survive the feelings that flowed. The intensity of them engulfed me.

Within a few days of that hospital transfer, we were told by one of Joani's doctors that Joani was not expected to live. Her fever was destroying vital brain function, and other organs were being compromised as well. I went numb in my emotions. I stopped the flow of feelings; I did not go to the hospital. If God was going to take her little life, I wanted my last memory to be of the stolen moments I had of touching her hair and feeling the baby softness of her skin. Sometime after that phone call, little Joani entered the portals of heaven.

Now, here's where I judge myself, Luci, and where I lost inner freedom. I needed to go to the hospital and see her again, even if the sight of tubes and respiratory equipment devastated me. I needed to finally hold her. I needed to get closure on that heart-wrenching experience. But that did not happen because I chose to protect myself from the flow of my intense emotion. I did not want to see Joani's final chapter. I did not want to feel it. So I shut down.

LUCI: *Oh, honey! That story makes me cry. I so hate that pain for you. But I have to admit, I don't quite understand how your responses to Joani's death interfered with your inner freedom.*

MARILYN: I stopped my emotions before they finished. I didn't allow myself to feel the death phase of that experience. I felt the grief of her physical challenge and my pain in it, but there was more I needed to feel. I protected myself from it because I didn't think I could bear it. The result is that even now, forty-one years later, I regret that I did not see her before she died. I regret I did not hold her at least one time, even though her little spirit was then in heaven. I missed a major part of the reality of that baby life. I regret I did not let my emotions finish what they needed to do, which was to flow freely.

Luci: Well, Marilyn, aren't you talking about that word shrinks use: repression?

MARILYN: In many ways, yes. Repression may be the shutting down of memories, feelings, and thoughts that are so safely tucked away there is no remembrance of them to the conscious mind. All my memories are intact; I simply have some regret about what I clearly remember. I have not repressed those memories, or I would not continue to feel them so deeply.

PART 4

Free for a Lifetime

Marilyn Meberg and
Luci Swindoll

15

Understanding the
Bondage of Legalism

Receiving my God-given freedom

Marilyn Meberg

The survival of the human race depends on its ability to find new homes elsewhere in the universe because there's an increasing risk that a disaster will destroy earth. This ominous thought was communicated recently by the world-renowned physicist Stephen Hawking. He also said humans could have a permanent base on the moon in twenty years and a colony on Mars within the next forty years.

Were it not that Dr. Hawkins has no peers in his field

of physics, I might be tempted to whisper, "That's cuckoo!" But because he has the most brilliant scientific mind living today, instead of whispering, "Cuckoo!" I simply cock my head and whisper, "No way."

Similarly, it does not seem improbable to me that the earth risks a disaster that could destroy it, but even so I still whisper, "No way!" Somehow my brain cannot wrap itself around the destruction of the earth. Not only do I have difficulty thinking about the earth's end, I cannot imagine pulling up stakes and moving to another planet. The whole idea is bigger than my mind can sit with.

And yet I find a good many biblically clear-cut facts about God that are bigger than my mind can sit with. For instance, I cannot imagine why God is more interested in me than in what I can do for Him. My reasoning is that simply loving God does not get the job done; working does. But Romans 4:4 says, "When people work, their wages are not a gift. Workers earn what they receive. But people are declared righteous because of their faith, not because of their work" (NLT). Getting the job done is not as important as the faith of the one doing the job.

Another fact about God that is bigger than my mind can sit with is that He does not stop loving me when I completely blow it. When I behave like the prodigal son, dishonor the name of my Father, and choose sin over love for Him, He does not abandon me. He looks for me to return to His arms and the security of His unconditional love. Dare we say that fact is cuckoo? Dare we say that kind of love makes as much sense as looking for a cute little house on Mars?

MIND-BOGGLING BUT TRUE

With all due respect, God's ways don't make sense to me most of the time; they stretch my mind beyond what I can comfortably sit with. Scripture says God's ways are not my ways, and that's why being chosen by Him does not always make sense to me. He is more interested in who I am than what I do, and He does not leave me when I leave Him. Those two major characteristics of God's person are mind-boggling. So what do people do with those characteristics when they don't make sense? Often they reinterpret them until they *do* make sense. What makes sense to most people is performance. So if God can be interpreted as One who values performance more than person, it makes more human sense and requires less faith.

The performance person may agree that faith is important, but his or her life's emphasis is not faith but works. That person's primary consideration is how many committee meetings are on the calendar, how many World Vision orphans are adopted, how much money is being tithed, how many shoes are going to the shoeless, and how many mission trips can be scheduled. The performance-oriented person quotes that handy verse from James that says "faith without works" is useless. Then he or she sits back and thinks, *I'm sure this is what God wants from me.*

What God wants from us first is our heart, not our performance. Often the performance person doesn't have the faith to believe God is able to love unconditionally. The performance person feels God will be inspired to greater love by our greater good deeds. Titus 3:5 reminds us, "He saved us, not because of righteous things we had done, but because of his mercy."

Those of you well-schooled in Scripture know that Jesus had little patience with the Pharisees, a group of people who prided themselves on piety and righteous living. They had enlarged the Ten Commandments by adding hundreds of addendums so that freedom and joy in living out their faith were nonexistent. The Pharisees heartlessly accused Jesus of working on the Sabbath because He healed a man with a withered arm on that day. Jesus looked at them in anger (see Mark 3:5). He said in John 10:10, "I am come that they might have life, and that they might have it more abundantly" (KJV).

There is no freedom or abundant living when we are madly going about in an effort to win the love of God. That love has already been won. There is no freedom or abundant life when we struggle with keeping laws, rules, and regulations.

When my mother left her agnostic mind-set and came into an understanding of Jesus and the salvation He offers, she was totally committed. Unfortunately, a band of very narrow-minded persons took my mother aside and began training her in how to renounce the "ways of the world": no cosmetics, no perfume, no short-sleeved blouses, no movies, no dancing, and certainly no fun! She took it seriously and complied with all their "rules." Years later, she realized she had been severely influenced by a group of modern-day Pharisees to whom the letter of the law mattered more than the freedom found in Jesus.

THE SUBTLETY OF PHARISAICAL THINKING

In many ways, pharisaical thinking is subtle and can creep up on the conscientious believer without detection. When we become more interested in what is "allowed" and not "allowed," we are in danger of the rigid inflexibility of pharisaical thinking. When we realize we are known more for what we are against than what we are for, we may be falling into the Pharisee camp.

How can you know if you are a performance person with pharisaical tendencies? I suggest you do an inventory on yourself. Have you allowed rules to rule you? Do you feel the need to correct rather than to support? Are you more comfortable doing work than receiving love? Are you trying to gain God's favor by keeping rules?

If you fall into those thinking traps, choose to get out of them. God chooses freedom for us, not bondage. Second Corinthians 3:17 tells us, "The Lord is the Spirit, and where the Spirit of the Lord is, there is freedom." We have the Spirit of the Lord living within us. That means the freedom of the Lord is also within us. Our task is to avoid the performance trap and live the abundant, free life Jesus came to give us. That's a choice we can clearly decide upon this very minute.

For those who continue to choose bondage over freedom, perhaps we might interest them in property on either the moon or Mars.

16

Exchanging the Bondage of Legalism for the Liberty of Grace

Giving your life away in service to others brings true freedom, inside and out

Luci Swindoll

I've always loved the sixth verse of James, which reads, "He gives us more grace." Isn't it the truth? He pours it on when we least expect it.

One day about twenty years ago my friend Paul received by mistake at his place of business six thousand dollars worth of Godiva chocolate. It was delivered there by an American Airlines truck. Because he happened to be in the shipping-and-receiving area when the truck arrived, Paul was asked to sign for the delivery, which he did. Then the truck drove off. Once he realized what he had on his hands, Paul went straight to his boss and asked if the chocolate was a legitimate order. When he was told it wasn't, he called American Airlines to please come back and pick it up. But guess what. The airline refused!

Being an upstanding young man of moral character, Paul decided to call the headquarters of Godiva Chocolatier in New York. He told them that several hundred pounds of chocolate had been mistakenly dropped off at his loading dock by American Airlines and he had requested that they come back and get it, but the airline said they couldn't. "What should I do now?" he asked. "I just wanted you to know it's here so you could send a carrier service to pick it up. It's all waiting for you. Nothing has been touched."

After a few moments, the person on the other end of the line said, "It's too difficult for us to pick it up, too complicated. Just keep it. Share it with your friends and enjoy it."

Needless to say, Paul was stunned. And he was *beside himself* with joy.

His mother, Judy (one of my very close friends), called me about an hour later almost yelling into the phone with excitement, "Luci, you're not going to believe this:

Paul just called to tell me a ton of Godiva chocolate has been delivered to his office by mistake. When he tried to return it, nobody would take it. He's got boxes and boxes of chocolate coming out his ears. Want to come over for coffee after a while and help us eat it? He said we could have all we wanted."

We ate chocolate for weeks and weeks, Judy, Paul, and I. Paul even gave me my own stash so I could slowly eat my weight in those little heavenly bars. Godiva chocolate is one of my favorite things in the world, and it takes me forever to eat one piece. I savor it and carry on and moan and enjoy it to the hilt. That's what I did with that wonderful gift.

Ironically, a few months before this mistake happened, I had bought a box of Godivas, and upon opening it, I saw that one piece right on top was missing. I was *sick.* I promptly reported it to the store it came from, thinking they'd give me a free pound, but they didn't. They sent me a tiny Godiva cloth patch, I suppose to sew on my shirt so everyone would know I was an addict. Oh, well, this recent load made up for that small disappointment.

FREED BY GOD'S GENEROUS GIFT OF GRACE

This story is a perfect picture of what grace is all about, my friends. Put yourself in my friend Paul's place with this windfall: he didn't expect it . . . didn't earn it . . . didn't deserve it . . . and he couldn't return it. It was literally dropped on his doorstep with the encouragement to share it with his friends and enjoy it. How cool is that? That's exactly what God does with His amazing grace. He gives it with no strings attached. He doesn't operate out of what we think He owes us. He operates out of His heart of generosity. Godiva owed me one little piece of chocolate and the company wouldn't pay up; the company owed Paul nothing and he got the whole, unexpected truckload.

Accepting the gift of grace that God has given us sets us free, both inside and out: free to be ourselves and let others be themselves; free from worry, shame, remorse, and fear; free for His service wherever He takes us. Freedom *to*, freedom *from*, and freedom *for*. He covers it all through grace.

When I want to read about true freedom, I always turn to the book of Galatians. Martin Luther, the great advocate of the Protestant Reformation, believed it to be the best book in the Bible. He said he was "in wedlock" with this book. Everything about it affirms our liberty in Christ. In my view, there's not a better book pointing to freedom than Galatians. It shows us who we are within and without. My brother Chuck says in *The Living Insights Study Bible*,

Galatians is a forceful, potent pronouncement of freedom based on grace. It is a letter celebrating the freedom we find only in Jesus Christ—not freedom to do whatever we please, but freedom from sin and freedom to obey and serve our Savior.[1]

It has been our desire in this book to encourage you to embrace wholeheartedly the liberty we have in Christ. In the thirty-four years I've known Marilyn, one of our favorite topics of discussion has been and continues to be freedom. We've encouraged each other to be who we are inside . . . our own person. Just as I have always wanted Marilyn to choose for herself what she wanted to do, how she wanted to live, where she wanted to go, and when she wanted to say yes or no, she's always encouraged me to do the same. Even in our times of disagreement, we've maintained a strong, loving relationship of interdependence and freedom. What a wonderful, liberating friendship we've enjoyed all these years! And in this book it's been our pleasure to share our thoughts and beliefs with you.

God has given every one of us a truckload of freedom through grace, all paid for by our Savior, Jesus Christ. We didn't expect it, didn't earn it, didn't deserve it, and can't return it. So, why don't we just receive it and enjoy it?

NOTES

Chapter 1.

1. Henri Nouwen, *The Road to Daybreak* (London: Darton, Longman & Todd Ltd., 1997).

Chapter 2.

1. Elie Wiesel, Nobel Peace Prize Acceptance Speech, 1986, © The Nobel Foundation.
2. Ibid.
3. Ibid.

Chapter 7. Giving Because You've Been Given To

1. Stephen Olford, *The Grace of Giving* (Memphis: Encounter Ministries, 1972), 94.
2. A. W. Tozer, *The Alliance Witness*, October 8, 1958. Used by permission.
3. World Vision India mission statement. www.worldvision.org.

Chapter 8. Choosing Between Yes and No

1. Daniel Taylor, *Myth of Certainty* (Downers Grove, IL: Intervarsity Press, 2000). Used by permission of InterVarsity Press, PO Box 1400, Downers Grove, IL 60515. www.ivpress.com.
2. Ibid.

Chapter 9. Learning to Wait Instead of Running Ahead

1. Malcolm Gladwell, *Blink: The Power of Thinking without Thinking* (New York: Little, Brown, 2005), 15, 16.

Chapter 10. Receiving More When you Already Have Enough

1. E. H. Gombrich, *The Story of Art*, 15th ed. (London: Phaidon Press, 1995), 36.

Chapter 11. Knowing Beyond the Shadow of a Doubt

1. Jan Silvious, *Big Girls Don't Whine: Getting On with the Great Life God Intends* (Nashville: W Publishing Group, 2003), x.

Chapter 16. Exchanging the Bondage of Legalism for the Liberty of Grace

1. Chuck Swindoll, gen. ed., *The Living Insights Study Bible* (Grand Rapids: Zondervan, 1996), 1245.

CPSIA information can be obtained at www.ICGtesting.com
Printed in the USA
LVOW10s0523270114

370983LV00006BA/26/P